An Ultra Marathoner's Journey

As Hope Springs Eternal on Trails to the Finish Line

BY JACK ANDRISH

The opinions expressed herein are those of the author, who assumes complete and sole responsibility for them, and do not necessarily represent the views of the publisher or its agents.

All Rights Reserved
Copyright © 2021 by Jack Andrish

No part of this book may be reproduced or transmitted, downloaded, distributed, reverse engineered, or stored in or introduced into any information storage and retrieval system, in any form or by any means, including photocopying and recording, whether electronic or mechanical, now known or hereinafter invented without permission in writing from the publisher.

Dorrance Publishing Co
585 Alpha Drive
Suite 103
Pittsburgh, PA 15238
Visit our website at www.dorrancebookstore.com

ISBN: 978-1-6386-7143-5
eISBN: 978-1-6386-7678-2

Table of Contents

Prologue ix
Introduction xi

A Return to Running 1
The Mystical Experience 3
2001 5
2003 11
2004 15
2004 23
2005 29
2006 33
2006 41
2007 47
2008 53
2009 57
2011 63
2012 67
2015 71
2015 77
2016 87
2018 89

Poems, Reflections, and Other Stuff 93

Dedication

This book is dedicated to my wife Sue Ellen, my son Sean who introduced me to trail running, my daughter Shannon, my son-in-law Jamil, and my two granddaughters, Kaitlin and Allison. All of whom have traveled the trails of ultras with me as well as by themselves, on the way to their own "mystical experience" that comes with ultra running.

About the Author

I am now seventy-seven years old and am one of those "old runners." While I learned to run marathons during my forties (along with my wife, son, and daughter), it was not until I was fifty-five that I, along with my wife, son, and daughter, discovered trail running. For the past twenty years I was lucky enough to run ultra marathons, mostly mountain trail ultras from 50K to 100 miles. Following each effort to complete a 100 miler, I would write a "race report" which was mostly an emotional decompression. And along the way, mostly during a solitary training run, I would have an occasional inspiration for a poem or vignette.

I would share some of these "reports" and vignettes with family and a few friends and would be told "you should make a book." Now I am not a noted runner. I would struggle to even finish and most of my 100-mile attempts were just that, attempts only. So there is no name recognition for me except for a few in my local community. And I have never published a book, although I am fairly well-published in orthopaedic journals and a few medical books.

So what is my purpose for organizing this book? It is to share the "mystical experience" that I have found while running trail ultra marathons.

Prologue

Oh my. It doesn't seem that long ago that I would watch an old man running and wonder, why subject yourself to such strain (and embarrassment)? It would hardly look like running and certainly did not appear to be any fun. He would be so stiff and so slow; feet hardly clearing the running surface. But now I am that man. I am slow. I am stiff. I must concentrate on every step to "pick up my feet." Cracks in the pavement that used to be invisible are now land mines just waiting to cause me to trip and fall. Oh yes falls. Falls used to be just a part of running; especially trail running. A colleague once told me that trail running was a contact sport. "If you run trails, you will make contact with the ground." But as we age, the spontaneous "tuck and roll" becomes a splat! We fall harder as we age. So why does that old man "run?" Why? Because I am now that old man, I understand. It is a refusal to lose what once was a passion filled with enjoyment and a feeling of accomplishment. And, secretly, it is an unspoken hope that practice will bring improvement. It is the understanding that if we don't try, we will surely lose all ability to run at all. And then, forgetting about our pace and times, comes the feeling (and joy) of accomplishment. We do what we can do and be thankful for that!

So what is the bottom line? To the "young" the old man running will always be an enigma. How can the young understand? It is unfair to expect anything else. But with time and the inevitability of our diminishing skills comes empathy and understanding. Enjoy (or maybe I should say "accept") the opportunities of aging as well as of youth!

Introduction

It has been almost two decades since I crossed the finish line at the Western States 100. What went before and what came after for me I think is typical of most of the "mid-pack runners" and especially the "back of the pack" runners. Each and every runner, whether those at the front or those of us at the back, have individual mountains to climb, fears to over-come, and a sheer determination (and yes, courage) to carry on as far as our feet can manage. Perhaps more than anything else that is needed to get to the finish line of an ultra (technically any distance over the marathon distance of 26.2 miles, but more commonly 50 kilometers, 50 miles, 100 kilometers, 100 miles, and even more) is the conviction that one really, REALLY wants to finish. Without that determination there are just too many voices in our minds, during the inevitable lows that develop, telling us to stop. Telling us "It is okay" to stop. That it is "the right thing to do" to stop. Overcoming those voices is perhaps the most important thing needed to continue on in spite of our internal messaging.

I suppose it would be helpful to understand a bit about my background. Growing up in Kansas, sports were my passion. I was good enough as a kid to be respectable in football, basketball, and baseball, but mostly because of my enthusiasm for participation, not talent. That said, as commonly encountered in youth, my assessment of my own talent was inflated and based more on my own perceptions rather than reality. But whether reality or not, I was able to succeed in most sports at that early level except for one. That one was track. Oh my did I try. Growing up in Kansas and the home of numerous Native

American athletes, I was once told, anecdotally, that the reason they were so fast was that they "toed-in" when they ran. Who knows where that came from, but realizing that my athletic future would be enhanced if I could run faster, I tried. And I tried, and I tried. But whether I toed-in or toed-out or just forgot about my foot strike all together, I was just hopelessly slow. Moments in life can bring dreams back down to reality and for me, two episodes stand out in my memory. The first was in middle school football practice where we were paired up for timed wind sprints. I was only perhaps 110 pounds at the time and my competitor-teammate was over three hundred pounds. And it wasn't even close. Losing to him was a shock to my self-esteem, but not a deterrent. The second memory I have, also in middle school, was desperately trying to find something in track where I could at least be acceptable. I recruited a friend to go to our local track with me and try to run a mile. He was a friend, but not an athlete that I feared and certainly not a "runner." That said, we were off and running for the first of four laps. Not understanding the concept of pace, I sprinted forward only to succumb quickly into a "run" and eventually into a gasping slog. I still remember calling out to my friend to slow down and "wait-up." I did finish that mile, but never again to even think about distance running. As for my other "passions" of football and basketball, my lack of size and talent finally overshadowed my modest smarts, and I became a golfer!

An Ultra Marathoner's Journey

A Return to Running

Fast forward, my wife and I agree that our twenties were a blur. Married at age twenty-one, the next decade was fully occupied by medical school, residency and fellowship training, and starting a family. We graduated from Ohio University at age twenty-one and woke up in our thirties. It was in our thirties that both my wife and I became recruited into "jogging." For a few years I would run twenty minutes a few times a week and felt that was enough for cardiovascular health. And maybe it was, but one day my wife and I observed a 10K run that was organized by our local community. The runners came right by our home, and it was inspiring. We both determined to get out of our comfort zone and run that race the following year. And we did. We came in dead-last, but we ran our first 10K and actually felt good about the experience.

Now you should know that the talent in our family has come from my wife, not me. She was a beautiful runner and went on to win her age group in several races. But to get back to my transition into running, I continued at this modest level until age forty-three. I had often thought about how special it would be if I could only run and complete a full marathon. I had considered this task to be out of reach for me because of the time it would take to train and there was barely enough time in the day for my work and my family. But one day changed that. While relating my wish to run a marathon to a friend who actually did run marathons, he steered me to the writings of Jeff Galloway who gave a plan to safely run and complete a marathon in three months following the ability to run 8 miles comfortably. And it worked! For the next ten years we ran two marathons a year, spring and fall. We have special memories with marathons from Columbus to Cleveland to DC to Boston to New York to Bordeaux and even Tromso, Norway. But as much fun as we had with marathons, running was never the end-all. Primarily, we ran marathons to be able to maintain a level of conditioning that enabled us to do what we really enjoyed, bicycle touring and skiing (downhill and backcountry). And that was a great time of our lives. As our son and daughter grew and transitioned through college and graduate schools, we recruited them into the joys of distance running as well.

Now we enter into our introduction to trail running. My son was in graduate school in Arizona and had joined a group of runners that got into trail running. During one of our visits, he insisted that I come out to run one of the many desert trails around Tucson. I did and I still have one of the prickly pear thorns embedded in my knee to prove it. But as time would tell, he went on to run a local Arizona 50K race that went from the desert floor to a mountain top and of course he insisted that I try the following year. That race became my first "ultra." I struggled, of course, but completed just within the official time. And I was hooked. The following year my wife and I both ran that ultra and the year after that, my daughter. I think my son won that race three years in a row, but that is another story.

And so trail running soon became the passion that I never had for road running. It was great and proved amazing to experience where our two feet could take us. It was mystical! I should also note that when we were actively involved with trail ultras, it was then still a small community. Some would have said "a small community of nut cases." But in reality, it was (and still is) a very non-judgmental, inclusive community. We looked forward to revisiting with our community at the various races that were then not difficult to enter. So many events now require a lottery system to gain entry. Much has changed in ultra running over the past twenty years, but also so much remains the same. Once we get to the starting line, it is simply "one foot after another" for as long as we can manage. And it still provides such a special opportunity to explore and treasure the regions of natural beauty that our country offers.

The Mystical Experience

It was after running a few ultras of 50K and 50 miles that I came across an issue of *Marathon and Beyond* that was devoted entirely to the history of the Western States 100 Mile Endurance Run. Originally this 100-mile race through the mountains on the Western States Trail was a horse race called the Tevis Cup. The goal was to complete the course in one twenty-four hour day. Gordy Ainsleigh had completed the event before on his horse, but in 1974 with his horse being lame, he decided to just run himself. He did and completed the run within twenty-four hours. The rest is history. I was captured! If only I could complete a hundred miles running through the Sierra Nevada Mountains, THAT would be unbelievable. And so the dream to run and complete the Western States 100 became my quest and my passion. Along the way I was introduced to a great community of trail runners.

It is almost impossible to run ultras and reminisce without becoming emotional at some point. As I would pursue attempts to run and complete 100 miles, I would try afterward to put my emotions and reflections in print. Often as not I would record the experience while at thirty-five thousand feet traveling home from an event. And as you will see, my "successes" were far outnumbered by my DNFs (did not finish). But my love of the sport and unwillingness to accept my shortcomings are reflected in the many musings and poems that reflect that very long road to the acceptance of what I am still able to do and what I was fortunate enough to have once been able to do.

2001

The Western States 100

It was during my fifties that I got the bug for trail running and the dream of running the Western States 100. My first attempt was at age fifty-seven. In those days it was relatively easy to gain entry into the Western States 100, about a 50:50 chance if one passed the modest qualifying criteria. So, I naively submitted my application and was accepted! My ultra running resume at that time included three 50K races, two 50-mile races, and no 100-mile events. So I approached the starting line of the 2001 Western States 100 with no real clue about the "how to" run 100 miles through the Sierra Mountains. I knew that I would have to increase my weekly mileage in preparation for the big event. But I failed to recognize the importance of training for the terrain of the race. And since most of my background was still with road running, I would include weekend runs of up to 50 miles, but 50 miles on roads. As race-day approached I realized that I had no idea how to pace myself to go 100 miles and I really had no idea of the hazards and obstacles I would face. I was panicked. Somewhere I had heard that blisters would be a problem and that taping one's toes could be a preventative measure. And so the afternoon before the race I meticulously wrapped duck-tape around every single one of my toes, every one! Since the start of the Western States 100 begins at five AM, I tried to go to sleep at nine PM. I tried, but my heart was racing so fast and my adrenaline levels were so high that I literally had to pee every ten to fifteen minutes all night long! By three AM when the alarm rang, I was simply exhausted.

It is not an exaggeration to say that I was terrified as I approached the start of the 2001 Western States 100 Mile Endurance Run. I remember the thrill of the first climb out of Squaw Valley. I remember the legendary Gordy Ainsleigh (the first person to run and complete the race) passing me as we approached the top of the climb. But the rest of my day was a blur of insecurity. "What was the right pace? Oh my, how do I maintain a pace running downhill over rocks and roots?" The first time I realized that I was in jeopardy of missing a time cut-off was at Robinson Flat, about 30 miles into the run. At Western States, a warning horn is blown a few minutes before the time cut-off and then a second time at the cut-off. If one is not out of the aid station before the second horn, the runner is declared DNF and pulled from the course. For me, I heard the first horn but was able to move through the aid station before the second horn. As I moved on to the next aid station, I was told that I could even walk to the station before the cut-off. That was a bit reassuring, but I "ran" most of it anyway. And so I vividly remember the warning sounds as I approached Miller's Defeat (34 miles) and was pulled from the race for missing the time cut-off. It is also not an exaggeration to say that I was devastated! All of my physical preparation and dreams of finishing were abruptly ended. I was crushed.

But my dream of finishing the Western States 100 did not end at Miller's Defeat. It became not only a dream, but an obsession. What I learned from my first attempt at running 100 miles was that the training is not just about the miles, but it was learning to run on the terrain of the course. I needed to learn how to carry a pace on the downhills on single-track trails and to maintain some degree of pace on extended climbs. Cleveland is blessed to have hundreds of trails in close proximity, including those of the Cuyahoga Valley National Park. And many of those trails are filled with rocks and roots and climbs and descents. So when I was accepted into the 2002 Western States 100, I was better prepared, but not well enough. One of the many things I have enjoyed from the ultra running experience was the opportunity to learn about myself and to develop the tools needed to sustain an effort up to thirty hours (or more). Running ultras is a continual learning experience. My second attempt at Western States was not the panic of the first attempt. My wife Sue Ellen joined me at Michigan Bluff (55 miles) where I was hyper-ventilating and in some sort of metabolic imbalance. With some "tough love" she paced me to Forrest Hill (mile 62) where my daughter Shannon took over the pacing duties and we were able to make it to the Rucky Chucky river crossing of the

American River (mile 78) just before the cut-off time. We were the last ones to be allowed to move on. Oh how I had dreamed of crossing the American River at the Rucky Chucky crossing. Training over the trails about Cleveland and splashing through streams that to me were the same as crossing the American River, gave a reinforcement to my dreams. But as I dipped my feet into the water, the pain was enormous! Blisters suddenly dipped into ice cold water, sting! There went one reality check. And so I failed to arrive at the next aid station (Green Gate, mile 79.8) before time ran out. This time I was disappointed, but not devastated. I was just really tired.

Jack Andrish

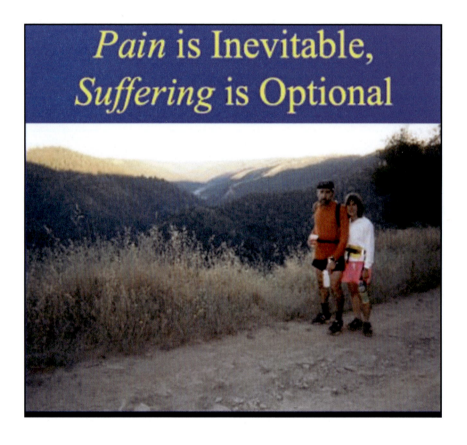

Cougar Rock, Western States 100

2003

It was during this phase of my life that my son also recruited me to the idea of running the Wasatch Front 100 Mile Endurance Run. "Dad, that is one of the classic 100 milers and is really, really tough." Oh why not? I had now been able to traverse 80 miles of the Western States 100. I was tested and after all, the Wasatch Front 100 had a thirty-six hour time limit; no problem!

Wasatch...A Rambling Account

Well, here I am at thirty thousand feet and contemplating another "ultra experience." Some things change and some things don't. My second try at a Western States 100 resulted in another DNF. But what an adventure! I don't know, maybe I'm just an 80 miler (I just completed the Wasatch Front 80 miler?...wrong, I DNF'd the Wasatch 100 miler).

But despite the predictable and the unpredictable, it was a weekend filled with a ton of good memories. To begin, the Wasatch course is simply spectacular! I couldn't believe where we were running, climbing, and scratching up and down mountain slopes. This course is definitely not for those prone to vertigo. The whole day (and then the next day too) was filled with spectacular scenery. As Shannon mentioned, "it was like being IN a picture." For starters, the race begins with a five thousand foot climb, ending up a final "assault" upon "Chinscraper." I had of course heard the talk of Chinscraper (a shear face of granite towering at nine thousand feet), but I'm thankful it was in the beginning of the run when we still had "fresh" legs. I was amazed that anyone would even think of including this in part of a trail run course.

Shannon was able to join us at the last moment and that made for a very special time. She and Sue Ellen were able to crew for Sean and me; what a difference that made. As for Sean, (who has partially controlled epilepsy) he has always felt something special about this race and would like to do well someday (like win or at least be in contention) but this was not to be the year. He was in the lead and then had his first seizure; a small one, but it rendered him a bit confused for a while. But he got back on track and was "reeling in" the leader (who had passed him when he got lost during the first episode) only to have a second seizure on the Lambs Canyon stretch. This one took him a half hour to "recover" but got him concerned because darkness was just ahead and he was now apprehensive about running this without a pacer (he had none) so he made the right decision and dropped out. He was disappointed to have dropped, but relieved I think to have come through it unharmed. The moral to this, of course, is that for extended runs he really needs to have someone (a pacer) with him.

As for me, I'm still learning. Thank goodness I'm young and still have so much potential! My goal was to finish in "Badger time" (thirty-six hours). And now after experiencing this race, I can understand that their "cut-off" times are very generous indeed. Although the course is more difficult than WS, no one there is intent upon pulling a runner off the course unless they are clearly delirious and a danger to themselves. But this time I was "metabolically" the best I have ever been. I think I may have an electrolyte and nutrition system that is reasonable for me. And my legs did not fail me (amazing with all of the climbing and steep descents). But my Achilles' heel this time were the monster blisters I developed around 50 miles that eventually made it difficult for me to run and miserable on the descents. I hate to be a wimp about a few blisters, but so be it. But I did make about 83-plus miles before I gave up the ghost, so to speak.

But what a great day anyway! Sue Ellen paced me for the three thousand feet of climbing up Lambs Canyon (53 miles, in darkness of course). We had a great time and even had a fellow traveler for a while that we think was a large cat (mountain lion versus cougar). This was on the descent portion of that section and I was stimulated to pick up my pace, but I was a good husband and kept calling for Sue Ellen who was behind me with the cougar to ask if she was all right! Then Shannon paced me up the way to Desolation Lake (67 miles); now this went down in the memory bank as special. Our ascent up to the Desolation Lake aid station was uneventful except we could see the sky flash occasionally (lightning?). Then, after leaving the aid station, we were climbing up the circ, which is the top of the Alta ski area I believe, when Shannon and I found out in spades what had been making the sky flash. Yes, we were at the highest point on the ascent, nothing but granite and a mile from the aid station, when we were caught in a typical western "big sky" thunderstorm. But at whatever elevation we were at the time (ten thousand feet?) the storm pelted us with hail, freezing rain, and even snow. The winds were fierce and Shannon and I were clueless as what to do. We didn't know where we were, nor did we know where we were going. The "trail" at this time was simply a pile of rocks on a mountain top. I must say, Shannon kept her cool much better than I did. The good news of course is that eventually the lightning passed and we could emerge from under the boulder we had been using for shelter and resume our trek (now in just a cold, cold rain), but the bad news is that I was ill-prepared. My twenty-year old "lucky jacket" that I had brought along as a windbreaker in case I needed it was no rain jacket! It immediately became a frozen, soaked shell intent on lowering my core body temperature into the twilight zone. Shannon was good for me here as she honed her medical skills by keeping me moving and up on fluids and nutrition (apparently needed for the treatment of hypothermia). On the way down from Scott's aid station I rallied from hypothermia, but my legs were now trashed and my blisters were overbearing. With the encouragement of Sean, Shannon, and Sue Ellen I took off from the Brighton Lodge aid station (75 miles), alone up and over Catherine's pass and Point Supreme, down into Ant Knoll and then up "the Grunt" and into the Pole Line aid station (83 miles) where it was clear that the final 16 to 17 miles with the steep descents were going to make it a very long way home.

So all in all, it was a beautiful extended weekend with family and enough good memories to last for another year. Oh yes, next year? How can one pass on the opportunity to do this again? And next year I'll be sixty. What could be better than finishing the Wasatch 100 in "Badger time!"

2004

Oh yes, sixty years old seemed like the "last chance" to complete a 100 miler. Little did I know just how real that opinion would be. But I did the obligatory qualifying for another WS 100 at the JFK 50 Mile and pointed my dreams and ambitions toward California.

The Western States 100
June 26/27, 2004
Life in a Parallel Universe
(On the way to the Rucky Chucky river crossing)

Well, it has taken me a lot longer this time to muster up my thoughts and impressions of my latest attempt at the Western States 100 Mile Endurance Run. In years past I have been in a state of emotion so extreme that the words just flowed while at thirty-five thousand feet on my way home. Not this time. I would say a state of mellowness would more aptly have applied to my ride home in 2004. But now, one week to the day later, I seem to have regained my emotional state of labiality and am ready to relate.

This quest, to complete the WS 100, has been a five-year journey. It began when I came upon an issue of *Marathon and Beyond* from the late nineties, which was devoted to the history and personalities of the WS. I was fascinated, captured, inspired. I'm no veteran ultra marathoner and at that time I was just learning about the sport from Sean. He had taken me on my first trail run while he was living in Tucson and I still have the "prickly pear" needles embedded in my right knee to prove it! But one thing leads to another and soon not only me, but Sue Ellen and Shannon were also on the trails of ultras from Arizona to Maryland. I suppose our family has a record of extrapolating success at one level into assumptions of success at other, much higher levels. ("Sure, since we have mastered the five-mile climbs of the Allegany State Park on our bicycles, of course we can cycle ourselves and eight of your high school friends across 1,500 miles of western outback from Montana to Kansas!") So the fact that my modest successes of a 50K in Arizona led to my determination to complete the "Boston" of ultra marathoning through the Sierra Nevada Mountains from Squaw Valley to Auburn, California was no surprise to me or anyone in my family. Boy was I naive!

I remember a quotation from G. K. Chesterton that could be aptly applied to my trail running experience, *"A man must love a thing very much if he not only practices it without any hope of fame and money, but even practices it without any hope of doing it well."*

And so, my attempt at the WS in 2001, which ended at Dusty Corners, 37 miles into the run; my "success" of completing the Rucky Chucky river crossing in 2002, only to be pulled off the course 2 miles later at Green Gate (79-plus miles); and my blistered ending last year after 83 miles of the Wasatch Front 100 Mile Endurance Run gave hope, but no guarantee for my third attempt at WS in 2004. But that said, it was great to be here in 2004! I had the best ever spring training for me. Sue Ellen had given me a Father's Day gift of attending the Memorial Weekend training runs on the WS course and my support crew for the race was great. Sean would help crew the first 55 to 62 miles then pace me the rest of the way (to the finish). A friend of his from Leesburg, Barbara Scott, was "just what the doctor ordered," calm and competent! And so on the morning of June 26, 2004, I and about four hundred of my "best friends" took off from Squaw Valley at five AM and made the climb to and over Emigrant Pass and into the "high country" portion of the Western States Trail. I fell early and skinned a knee, but my sturdy if not tank-like New Balance 1100s protected my previously broken big toe and the fall served as a wake-up call for me to pick up my feet! The first 30-plus miles of the course are truly beautiful with many vistas overlooking spectacular deep canyons and endless forest. Sue Ellen had been preaching to me (repeatedly!) over the spring that I could not be content with keeping within the thirty-hour pace, but I had to maintain a pace at least one hour below the thirty-hour pace. Of course she was not only right, but prophetic. I was able to maintain "check point" times that were forty-five to sixty minutes ahead of the thirty-hour pace through the first 62 miles! I even avoided crashing at my nemesis, Devil's Thumb (48 miles), and moved through the canyons ahead of schedule and into Forest Hill where Sean and Barbara were waiting to make the transition of Jack Andrish, solo runner, to the Jack and Sean team that would hopefully traverse the next 38 miles into the Placer County High School track and stadium finish. But the best laid plans of mice and men...or whatever...sort of fell apart at Forest Hill. The very efficient aid station visits I had been having succumbed to stumbling and bumbling at Forest Hill (62 miles). It was now dark and after finally successfully completing a change of shirts and reattaching all of my paraphernalia (camel-back, fanny pack, water bottles, etc.) Sean and I took off down California Street to re-enter the WS trail and move on to the 17-mile stretch of mostly downhill (apart from four modest climbs) to the Rucky Chucky crossing. We weren't on the trail for a hundred yards before my upset stomach became an urge to go number two! Sean told me to take the time now to "go" and it would be more than rewarded afterward. And so I made a detour off to the side of the trail and "prepared to go." I got out my tissues, took off my paraphernalia, and proceeded to squat. The problem was, I couldn't squat! After 62-plus miles of climbs and downhills, my quads wouldn't permit it. So now I had a dilemma that I had not prepared for; what to do? I tried to "go" standing up; ever try it? Not easy and I at least had no success. Then I spotted a tree stump (and oh yes, it was pitch dark at this point and only my flashlight could give me a clue of where I was). I had the inspiration to sort of back into the tree and then lower myself down against it; like the wall squats that I used to practice with my friend Gordon Bell while waiting for our patients to return from having x-rays. Well, it worked for a millisecond and then I found myself lying on my side, with my pants down, in the dark, with my fanny amidst leaves and critters, and I gave up. So be it. If I were to have diarrhea, I would have it while in the up-right position, while running on the trail to Rucky Chucky! After re-dressing I rejoined Sean on the trail and spent the next few miles picking sticks and who knows what else out of my pants while traversing, slowly, down the trail. And so it should have been no surprise that when we got to an aid station check-in point we were told that we were only fifteen minutes under the thirty-hour pace!

> *"A man must love a thing very much if he not only practices it without any hope of fame and money, but even practices it without any hope of doing it well."*
>
> (G. K. Chesterton)

Okay. I had lived those words long enough now! The warning we received at the Cal 2 aid station (70.7 miles) scared me! A fifteen-minute cushion was not enough to get me through the next 30-plus miles.

And this is where the *parallel universe* enters. As Sean and I left Cal 2, he gave me his headlamp, which was working much better than mine. I could see the trail. I started to run. I kept running, even on the up-hill sections. I ran the downhill, I ran the traverses, I ran the up-hills. I started passing groups of runners and their pacers. And they didn't catch up! *I had no pain.* It was mystical.

Sean and I arrived at the Rucky Chucky river crossing at three AM (78 miles); now fully one and a half hours under the thirty-hour pace. In the last 7 miles we had gained an hour and fifteen minutes of "cushion." We thought it was a mistake, a misprint of sorts, an aberration! To this moment, I don't know how we did it. It was mystical.

For the next 5 miles we maintained the pace and lead a pack of obviously superior runners (to me). We passed and were not passed. But then came a section, still in the dark, that entered a series of switchbacks uphill. With heads down and determined pacing we kept ahead of the pack. Trouble was, after about twenty minutes of serious climbing Sean recognized that it was "too quiet." I was in denial and swore I had seen a yellow ribbon just a few feet back, about thirty feet above us in a tree (I wonder how they tied it there?). I even saw a small black bear just ahead of us in the trail and scared him away with my flashlight (only to find out from Sean that it was no bear; it was a skunk!). And so we slowly reversed ourselves back downhill and sadly found out that we had missed a trail cut-off and had gone about thirty minutes out of our way (uphill, no less) and all of the "superior runners" we had been leading were far, far away. I think this was more of a psychological than a physical let down for me; but then at that point it is hard to separate the two. But we trudged on, and Sean now was invaluable in maintaining my spirits and my pace. Night became day and downhills became uphills. We made it to No Hands Bridge with a forty-five-minute "cushion" (96.8 miles) and for the last 3-plus miles I let myself believe that this time I just might make it all the way.

> *"A man must love a thing very much if he not only practices it without any hope of fame and money, but even practices it without any hope of doing it well."*
>
> (G. K. Chesterton)

After the last climb on the trail to get us out of the river valley and into the town of Auburn we met Barbara at Robie Point and celebrated the last mile into the Placer High School stadium. I admit to having trouble seeing everything and everyone as I broke through the entry onto the track. Tears have a way of doing that. Five years, more than a few DNFs, many hours of hill repeats in the Metro Parks of Cleveland, and now I had only 300 yards to go. With Sean by my side, Barbara along the infield, and what seemed like thousands of Virginia Happy Trails club runners and crew yelling encouragement, 300 yards soon became 100 yards, then 100 feet; then it was over. Twenty-nine hours, twenty-six minutes and twenty-six seconds and I had finished. I was now Jack Andrish, sixty years old and a *finisher* of the Western States 100.

Hooray! I made it to the finish line in time.

The Rucky Chucky crossing of the American River,
78 miles into the Western States 100 with the help of my son, Sean

2004

Trying to extend the joy of finishing WS, I was also accepted into the Wasatch Front 100 a second time; what an opportunity to celebrate being sixty. My whole family participated this time and shared the "mystical experience."

It takes a village.

Jack Andrish

On the Bubble Again: Wasatch Front 100, 2004

This has been quite a year for this aspiring ultra runner. After completing the Western States 100 earlier this summer (after two prior unsuccessful attempts), I was now poised to try the Wasatch Front 100. As my account from last year can testify, I had experienced the first 83 miles last year and was looking forward to experiencing the whole course this year. So as we lined up at five AM on a dark, desolate road in Kayesville, Utah with access to the Bonneville Trail, I remembered the starter's advice from last year, "Don't get lost; go!" Simple advice but to the point.

It's interesting how our memories can mercifully block out pain and effort. I had remembered the thrill of climbing "Chinscraper" and the surprise I had when I attempted to look back down the trail from the top and couldn't see it because of the steepness, but I somehow had forgotten the miles of climbing leading up to the Chinscraper Bowl following the initial 3 or 4 miles of the gentle rolling Bonneville Trail (which of course I *did* remember). And I had forgotten most of the ups and downs that followed, and I definitely had forgotten the briars and brambles and general scraggly brush that continually cut at my arms and legs. But once on top of the ridge, the next 40 miles of daylight provided the most spectacular views of the Wasatch mountain range, mountain meadows, aspen groves, as well as the Salt Lake Basin five thousand feet below. As my daughter Shannon had mentioned last year, it was like being *in* a picture.

Salt Lake City has had a very cool summer this year by their standards and no rain was forecasted for the weekend. Great! But the bad news was that Saturday was to be the hottest day of their summer and it was, with temperatures reaching ninety-four degrees. As a flatlander from Ohio, I would be expected to have some difficulty with the altitude but add to it the effects of heat and the result was a spectacularly beautiful but brutally harsh first 50 miles. My goal of course was to finish the course in Badger time of less than thirty-six hours. I had studied the split times for Badger and Cougar (thirty hour) times and I studied the "absolute cut-off" times for each aid station. And I had studied my "splits" from last year when my bubble finally burst at Pole Line (83 miles). Learning from my experience at Western States this year I now understood that to be actually running the Badger time splits was not enough of a cushion to accommodate the bad patches and the expected unexpected events that occur in the solitude of 100 miles of backcountry trail. I needed to be at least an hour ahead of Badger time splits.

And so I was a bit disappointed when my first recorded time was over Badger time and even ten minutes over my time last year. And I continued on that tardy pace throughout the day; not that I had any control over it. I struggled with the heat and my stomach. I came to hate GU, and electrolyte drinks, and even water! Nothing would stay down. I arrived at the 53-mile mark at Lamb's Canyon fifteen minutes behind last year's schedule (and an hour and fifteen minutes behind my hopes for this year). At Lamb's canyon, however, things got better. Sue Ellen and my son-in-law Jamil met me, poured chicken broth down me, and put a dry shirt and jacket on me and Jamil proceeded to be my first pacer. He was great. We marched up the three thousand feet climb of Lamb's Canyon trail and then ran down an idyllic trail joining a parallel stream and then up 3 miles of road to the Big Water aid station (62 miles) where Sue Ellen took over to nudge me up and over Desolation Lake, up to Scott's Peak, and then on to Brighton (75 miles). It was mystical!

In Brighton I found out that Sean had already finished and had run a good race. He did have problems with heat midway through the day and spent an hour and a half resting and rehydrating in the Alexander Ridge aid station, but he rallied and finished in 25:01; good for a tenth-place finish.

Between Jamil and Sue Ellen, I had made up forty-five minutes of time coming into Brighton and I believed (mistakenly) that I now had a thirty-minute "cushion." That illusion soon evaporated as some blister care and a change of clothes (and more chicken soup) devoured more time. My crew all told me that I "had a chance of making it" in time if I kept pushing. Kept pushing?! At this point I had just one speed (slow) with only one effort (maximum). So Shannon and I trudged out of Brighton in the daylight, up and over Catherine's Pass and more up and over Point Supreme. Then down. then up. then down, then up until I doubted my senses. "Surely it won't be this hard all the way to the end?"

I also became just a bit paranoid on this stretch. It began with Jamil telling me "I had a chance to make it" if I continued to push, with Sue Ellen repeating the mantra, and Shannon quietly, but firmly, continuing the routine. I became convinced (now supported by my "fuzzy logic") that they all had come up with the scheme to keep me in the dark on my true pace and probability of finishing by not telling me that in truth I had a comfortable cushion. And so, I continued to push the hills, but I had the belief that I had an hour or two cushion. (Should I push really hard and finish in thirty-four hours or "enjoy the day" and still finish in thirty-five hours?) Oh my.

Wasatch was beautiful. Life was good. I was struggling up the hills, but I was comforted in my belief that I was okay on time. We left the last aid station at Pot Bottom (93 miles) with two hours and fifteen minutes to cover 7 miles. By now my ability to calculate was totally shot, but not to fear. Shannon was still telling me that I had a chance to make it in time (Oh yeah, *wink, wink!*). And so we went up out of Pot Bottom looking for the last downhill trail out of the backcountry and into Midway. Okay. So now we had 3 miles of downhill and an hour to do it in. "A piece of cake!" Life was good. The aspens were absolutely beautiful! And then it happened. Ahead on the trail was Sue Ellen. Great. But she looked worried. She should look happy, joyous even. But she didn't. And then came Chris (Sean's friend and pacer from Tucson). Chris had run this race before and knew the course well. Chris looked concerned. What's going on here? The aspens were absolutely stunning and we should be skipping hand in hand into Midway together, celebrating a grand and glorious weekend in Wasatch. But we weren't. Instead, *everyone*, Shannon, Sue Ellen and even Chris were telling me that if I ran really hard, I could make it. Really hard? At 98 miles! Oh well, there are times in life that we really have no choice. We had come too far to miss this opportunity to finish in Badger time. Chris ran. Shannon ran. Sue Ellen ran. *I ran*. Oh my, when would we ever get off this (beautiful) trail and onto the road to Midway and the Homestead? My stomach hurt. I felt sick. I wanted sooo much to walk a bit, just a bit, but my pacers and crew wouldn't hear of it. We ran, probably faster than I had run at any point in the race. And still they wouldn't let up! "You have a chance to make it (only) if you keep running!" I'm sick. I'm dizzy. Oh my, we're off the trail and on the road, but my god where did this headwind come from? And now it's even raining! I can't see! My contacts, peltered by nearly thirty-six hours of heat and dust and no sleep have glued themselves to my eyeballs and have rendered me nearly blind. I follow Shannon onto the final grassy field leading to the finish line. Shannon pulls away to let me finish unfettered in victory. But I can't see. "Just run under the finish line."

"What finish line?"

"That finish line, under the white banner."

"What banner?" I can't see. I'm sick. I'm running. I'm going to vomit right here on this grassy field, somewhere in the vicinity of a white banner that is apparently the finishing line. "Shannon, don't leave me. Let me follow you to the finishing line. I can't see!"

I'm told that it was raining when we finished the 100 miles of the Wasatch Front last Saturday. I don't really remember that now. I can barely remember the nausea and fatigue of the last "sprint" to the finish. What I do remember are the cheers I heard from my friends of the VHTRC (they're everywhere!), the smile on Sue Ellen's face, the warmth of knowing Shannon and Jamil and Sean were there to share the day, finally being close enough to see the banner signifying "finish," and yes, the aspens. The aspens were spectacular!

—Jack Andrish, Finisher of the Wasatch Front 100 Mile Endurance Run 35:50:21

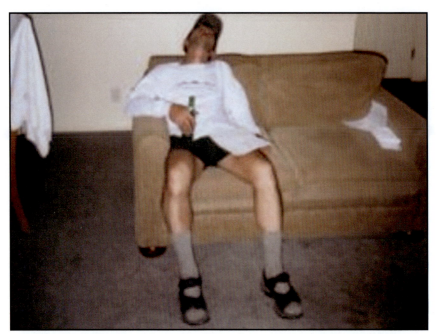
After finishing 100 miles over the Wasatch mountains, sleep trumped beer.

2005

How could I top that summer? I couldn't. But still having the legs and dreams, I continued to enjoy the participation in ultras. I would do five ultras a year; a couple of 50Ks and 50 milers (my favorites being Bull Run Run in Virginia and Old Pueblo in Arizona). But never again would I have the successes of my sixtieth year.

WHY AM I HERE?

Oh my, it's June 24th and I'm in line again for the check-in to the Western States 100. It seemed like only a month ago that my name had been drawn from the lottery. But that was December and many months ago. Many months of attempts to train for this adventure in the mountains and canyons of the Sierras. Attempts I say because through a conspiracy of injuries, travel commitments and weather, this winter/spring was my worst training for consistency. Did I say I lived in Cleveland where the year 2005 brought a record snowfall? Well, it did and for all of us in Northeast Ohio, it made the trail running a bit tough. And injuries; I sounded like patients from my own orthopaedic clinic. Start running, slow for snow. Start running, stop for foot pain (Oh, could this be a Jones type stress fracture?). Start running, slowed by hamstring pain (Oh my, could this be the time I would be unable to "run through it?"). Start running, stop for ankle pain (Oh no, not a medial malleolar stress fracture?). This was my winter/spring, until May. With May came hope. My training was more consistent and a few days running the hills and trails of Allegany State Park in New York made me feel a bit better about my chances in California. So here I am at the check-in, along with four hundred of my "closest friends." The energy level is thick. At weigh-in I'm up six pounds from last year; perhaps not a bad thing? And my blood pressure is up; no, it must be the altitude and the excitement. But I get my wristband with all of my "vitals" tattooed and it is official. I'm signed, sealed, and delivered for the start of the WS 100, June 25, 2005.

The morning of the start was cool but not cold. The trip up to Immigrant Pass was chilly, but not bad and the rest of the day would be unseasonably cool temperatures for the canyons and beyond. That was very good news. But did I mention the snow? This year the mountains around Tahoe received 150 percent of their usual annual snowfall, and it showed. Although not the "bad" snow years of the mid-nineties, there was still lots of snowpack to traverse for much of the first 20-plus miles of the course. And for "unsteady" runners like me, it was just another obstacle to muster through. One thing I've learned about myself from prior experiences is that I cannot afford to cut too close to the cut-off times. I need a "cushion" to help when adversity strikes. And adversity *will* strike everyone at some time during a 100 miler. The only variables are what and when and how we handle it. I suppose in some way that is part of the attraction. We know that physical and mental challenges await us and the hope is that we somehow will make good decisions and push beyond what can seem insurmountable. And so, my split times from last year, which I had carefully inscribed into a laminated card as my goals to meet or better this year, soon became a relic. Engulfed by the high country, I became insecure. Why am I here? Perhaps I am too old for this and perhaps I should put a stop to 100 milers, at least. Perhaps the time has come for me to hone my golf game.

After traversing the "High Country" of the Sierra mountains, the infamous canyons of the WS trail did not disappoint. Spared of the normal heat, however, they came and went with only "the usual" nausea and vomiting. I joined Sean for my pacer at Michigan Bluff (56 miles), sooner than I had hoped, but necessary because darkness was near and I was "behind." But Sean provided a lift to my spirits and we pushed on through Volcano Canyon, Forrest Hill, and onward to the Rucky Chucky river crossing (78 miles). Last year this stretch was my "mystical experience." It was mystical enough this year to the point that we had made up my lost time and arrived at the Rucky Chucky more than an hour ahead of the thirty-hour pace. The feeling of "comfort" however, was short lived. This year, because of high flows in the American River, runners were not allowed to cross by wading along a towline, but rather were ferried across in a raft. That was good for safety, but only four runners/pacers could use the raft at a time and the waiting time was nearly thirty minutes! So we waited in the middle of the night to cross the river and begin the final stages of the "run." It was about this time that I began to slow down; inconsequential at first, but little by little I was losing time.

And then came Auburn Lakes at about 85 miles. We moved through the aid station and Sean sent me ahead while he updated supplies. Almost immediately I came to a stream. Now that is not so bad. There had been plenty of streams to cross along the way, but I had developed open blisters on my left foot and the last crossing I had walked through had ignited such a fire in my foot that I was reluctant to repeat the feeling if I could avoid it. So I carefully eyed a path through the stream using a series of rocks and boulders. As I got to the other side, I had a dilemma. The stream bank was a good foot above the water and I had the choice to step up upon the bank from the boulder I was standing on or turn left and wade through the water to a more gently banked slope. I chose the former and stepped up. I soon knew I had made a bad decision. My quads were failing me and I starting teetering. I knew I was going to fall, but I was trying desperately to fall toward shore and not backward. I tried, but failed. It is somewhat mystical, I suppose, when accidents happen. Everything goes slow and fast at the same time! I could feel the fall, but then suddenly the boulder arose from the water and hit me in the jaw (and arm and chest and face)! I could feel the pain in my mandible and wondered how it could not be broken and how I would handle that. And then, instantly and simultaneously, I felt the pain in my head and wondered if I was going to get a subdural, or even worse, epidural hematoma. I lay there in the water as I did hear another runner yell back to me asking if I was "Okay." I was a bit stunned and just sat there until Sean came by and asked why I was lying in the stream. But he soon saw blood and realized that there had been an accident. So next comes the "self test." Okay, the jaw works; Okay, the arm works; Okay, the head seems clear; Okay, I can breathe; so let's go!

And so, as you can guess, the next and final 15 miles were a struggle. My legs were gone. My "run" was nothing more than the equivalent of a slow trot. Good walkers were blowing by my attempts at running. My right shoulder and chest hurt; my scoliosis was collapsing with my left rib cage painfully impinging into my pelvic brim. Oh yes, the blisters had not gone away either. I was ready to turn it in. I saw no way of continuing. I was beaten. But Sean would not let me quit (I was having delicious illusions of being rescued at the next aid station and finding a comfortable, warm bed; pain free!). Amazingly enough, we made the time cut-off at Brown's Bar at 90-plus miles and even more amazingly, we made the time cut-off at Highway 49 (93.5 miles); amazing to me because of the significant climb required to get up there. And then most amazing was that we got to No Hands Bridge in time to be allowed to finish. No Hands Bridge is only 3.5 miles from the end. Three and a half miles but with a last gasp climb out of the canyon floor. This time I had nothing left. I struggled up and into Auburn with the last mile ahead of me, now knowing I was not going to be an "official" finisher. But being a finisher in an "unofficial" way, nine minutes over the thirty-hour time limit, was fine by me at this point. We moved uphill and then down into the Pacer High stadium and track. I wasn't sure if I would be allowed to actually enter the track, but everyone was so kind. It was community! I could hear and see my friends from Ohio and my friends from Virginia (Happy Trails) and my friends from ultra running events not even from Ohio and Virginia. And it was clear that it mattered not that I was "unofficial." I had covered the distance as best I could. And that, after all, was why I was there in the first place; to cover the distance as best I could.

So now I'm at thirty thousand feet and on my way back to family and friends and work. Next year this time, I'll be sixty-two. And where will I be and what will I be doing on the last weekend in June?

Jack Andrish
June 27, 2005

2006

My son had been living in Leesburg, Virginia and working in DC for a decade. He had made a group of friends all living in a Washington DC neighborhood called Woodley. Together they called themselves members of the Woodley Ultra Society (WUS). Most all were also members of the Virginia Happy Trails Running Club (VHTRC), a fantastic society of trail runners that would traverse up and down the trails of the Blue Ridge Mountains with the centerpiece being the Massanutten Mountain. Their organized ultras included the Bull Run Run 50 miler and the very difficult and gnarly Massanutten Mountain Trail 100 (MMT 100). I had participated a few times in the BRR, but the MMT 100 seemed out of my reach because of its difficulty. My wife and I had crewed for our son Sean at the MMT 100, including the year that he won the race. So it was no surprise that I eventually tried to run the MMT 100.

Jack Andrish
May 16, 2006

THREE MILES

Three miles. Thirty years ago, when my wife and I began to run for fun and to gain a level of conditioning that would make our biking and skiing more enjoyable, 3 miles was plenty. We actually started with a 1-mile loop around the neighborhood and stuck with that for a year or two until we actually got the ambition to go further. And we did, *3 miles*; Lander Road to Meadow Hill to Sterncrest to home. Three miles and I thought that would forever be enough. Of course as time went on, 3 miles became six and eventually 26.2. And then one day Sean introduced us to the joy of trail running and "ultras." And so 26.2 became 30 and 50 and even 100 miles. One hundred miles. Three miles no longer even registered a blip on our running scale. Practically a non-event!

I was exposed to the Massanutten Mountain Trail 100 a few years ago as crew for my son Sean and as a volunteer at the finish line with "Bunny." It became obvious that this was a special event; special because of the VHTRC enthusiasm and support and special because of the rugged terrain of Massanutten Mountain. Yes, I learned early on that "Massanutten Rocks." It snuck into my mind that maybe someday I could be on the other side of the aid station, but with my limited skills, it was only a dream. But then I decided that this year I would try. At age sixty-two, my future opportunities are finite. So I signed up and began preparing in the Metro Parks of Cleveland. Yes, Cleveland does have some hills and excellent single-track trails, hundreds of miles actually, but certainly nothing to compare to the rockiness of Massanutten Mountain.

We arrived at Skyline Ranch on Friday in time for the check-in and the pre-race instructions. It was good to be a "runner" this time, but I also felt a bit sheepish and unproven. I don't really like rocks. I am not good on rocks. I'm marginal at this distance even on much less technical terrain. Why am I even doing this? I'm going to get squashed on a rock or tumble down a ridge. My confidence was pretty thin. And then to add to the equation, we were informed that there had been a fire on the southern part of the mountain and the course was rerouted. We now got to run Kerns Mountain (Sean had always told me that this was the toughest part of the course for him), twice!

The good news was, however, that I had a great crew! Sue Ellen, Sean, and John Nelson would be at the aid stations along the way and share the pacing when nighttime came. It could be a picnic, if the weather permitted. And the weather did, big time. The conditions were perfect the entire weekend with only a brief shower Sunday afternoon.

But back to the race; five AM Saturday and "we're off." Three miles of gentle rolling, mostly downhill road got us warmed up. And then we reached the first trailhead going up to Buzzard Rocks. The climb was modest, but once on top of the ridge the rocks were (to me) unbelievable! They were huge and sharp and at times it was impossible to even conceive a trail if not for the runners in front of me. After a few miles of maneuvering through this gnarly precipitous terrain I was reasonably sure my time was limited. How could I ever meet the aid station time cut-off limits? But to my surprise, as the aid stations passed, my time "cushion" was increasing. I actually felt good and moved cautiously through the rocky sections and tried my best to run what I could. As morning turned into afternoon I was whistling along to "Tommy" and "Momma Mia" on my iPod Shuffle and life was good!

By the time I arrived at the Picnic Area aid station (47 miles) I was two hours ahead of the time cut-off. Sean joined me shortly thereafter as I was on my way up Bird Knob (51 miles) and nighttime came as we rounded back toward Route 211 aid station (57 miles). We had a great time together. How special to run with family in an event like this and to feel in control enough to enjoy the experience. Without a doubt, through mile 65, this was my best ultra ever; certainly my best 100 ever. But as Sean passed me off to John Nelson at the start of Short Mountain, I began to fade.

I love trail running and ultra running. I love the camaraderie of the training runs with friends; I even love the hours of running alone listening to my breathing or the sounds of the forest or even the sounds of the Cleveland Indians losing another game to the dreaded Chicago White Sox! And I love the 100-mile distance. It stretches the limits of all of us, those of us with limited talent as well as the talented. But it is a fickle distance. There are so many opportunities out there for failure as well as success. We all know that the one sure thing about a 100-mile race is that something "bad" will happen and the big unknown is how we will accommodate and hopefully overcome. Our body is an engine and experience helps us keep this engine in metabolic homeostasis during these long and strenuous events; but "things happen" out there.

And so, as John and I maneuvered the rocks and ridgeline of Short Mountain I noticed my posture was becoming more stooped. John noticed too and astutely pointed out to me that I "was all crooked." I had back problems before in 100-mile events. The sequela of a spine infection at age nineteen had left me with scoliosis, which was decompensating with age (I've already lost three and a half inches in height over the years). But this now was becoming "the issue" of my MMT 100 experience. By the time I got off Short Mountain I was struggling. But then Sue Ellen took over pacing duties and we had the best time possible under the circumstances moving from Woodstock Tower (84 miles) to Powell's Fort (90 miles). She got me through by singing the "left-right-left-right-left" song. Those 5.7 miles went by quickly, but my posture was getting worse; much worse than it ever had before. I just could not stand straight, and my rib cage was compressing my pelvis. My stomach was "squished!" I was the human imitation of a pretzel. Sean took over pacing again at Powell's Fort and we headed up and over to Elizabeth furnace; 7 miles of which 3 were up and 4 were down. The final mile of climbing was on a boulder field that seemed to never end! As we began the descent I tried to carry a pace, but I could not sustain it. I could hardly walk a hundred yards without having to stop and bend/stretch my back and gasp for air. Those 4 miles traveling downhill to Elizabeth Furnace seemed like an eternity. It was the longest stretch I have ever experienced in total frustration. As we finally struggled into the aid station, Sue Ellen was there and had somehow found a walking stick for me to take for the final 3 miles. Three miles. It was only 3 miles; one steep uphill mile and two down into the grassy picnic area of the Skyline Ranch Resort, and the finish line. Just 3 miles. Three miles hardly counts at all, right? Heck, that's only up Lander Road, around Meadow Hill Drive, Sterncrest, and home. That's hardly enough to get warmed up. Wrong! I managed 97 miles of Massanutten Mountain's rocky, gnarly trails with spectacular over-looks of the Shenandoah Valley below only to succumb to my frailties at mile 97-plus.

So what did I learn from this adventure in the Blue Ridge? I learned how lucky I am to have family and friends that support my "running" and are able to share the highs and provide comfort in the lows (no I'm not going to say "failure," just "low"). And I learned what a beautiful event the MMT 100 really is; beautifully prepared and supported by the great folks of the Virginia Happy Trails Running Club and beautifully nestled in the rugged and spectacular trails of Massanutten Mountain. And yes, just 3 miles; perhaps there is a brace out there that can get me *just 3 more miles!*

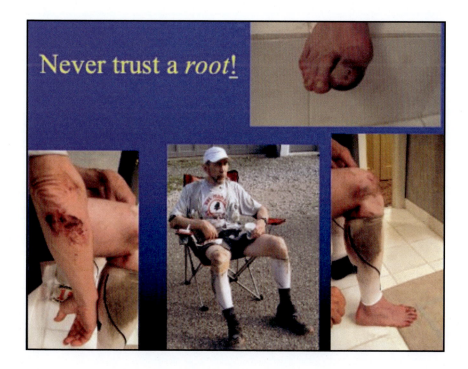

Massanutten Rocks!

The family affair at the Massanutten Mountain Trail 100 finish line.

2006

What can I say? Hope springs eternal. And Hope Pass was now calling me. Hope Pass outside of Leadville and home to the Leadville Trail 100 (LT 100). We had been playing in the mountains of Colorado for years, both summer and winter. My son would eventually move to Frisco, Colorado so it seemed natural that my "bucket list" would include the LT 100. But my age and diminishing skills were now becoming apparent. I had heard that the thirty-hour time limit was a hard stop for those of us who in the best of times would be at the back of the pack. You can't fake the effects of altitude.

The Thrill of Anticipation: Leadville Trail 100, 2006

Have you ever wanted a "do-over?" Of course you have; we all have had moments we wish we could do over again. Maybe even every day we wish we had a do-over; but then, sometimes we *really* wish we had, just one, "do-over."

Once again, I'm coming home from another attempt to run 100 miles. I'm now at thirty thousand feet and not tired, not stiff, and in no pain. What is wrong with this picture? I suppose it has something to do with the fact that my 100 miler turned out to be a 50 miler. "The Leadville 50" ... it has a nice ring to it, but the problem is, it was the Leadville 100. Oh well, I've never been accused of being a good runner; but I am a plodder and every now and then, the tortoise does succeed.

This summer was my opportunity to run two new (to me) trail ultras; the Massanutten Mountain Trail 100 and the Leadville Trail 100. My experience in

Virginia was wonderful, uplifting, and far above my expectations, until about the 70-mile mark when my physicality and especially my back, gave out. Ninety-seven miles of the MMT 100, however, left me with some hope, but also doubt. I spent the next two months experimenting with various back braces and found a few that I could tolerate while running and that seemed to help support my scoliotic spine. The best brace I found cost all of $8 (regularly $12). I found it on sale at the Middlefield Co-Op I visit every two weeks to get feed for my animals. I also tried several more expensive models that our orthotist at the Cleveland Clinic gave me, but the feed store model was far superior for this purpose.

And so our plans for Leadville continued this summer. In fact, "my Leadville" became not only my anticipation, but an anticipation for my wife, Sue Ellen as my crew "chief" (yes, "chief" implies that there would be more than one person willing to assume this role); my son, Sean as crew and possibly pacer, and then three "rookies" to ultra running who were eager to see first-hand just what this was all about. All three of my "rookie" friends are my partners at the Cleveland Clinic. John Bergfeld and Ken Marks were eager to be my "seconds" (as John B. would refer to the role of crew) and Tom Bauer, a budding ultra runner himself, was *really* looking forward to working crew and then to assume the role of pacer.

The summer went quickly, as it seems all summers do now that I have passed my sixth decade. Training runs through the Metro Parks and the Cuyahoga Valley National Park with my Cleveland friends and a few days with Sean, running through the Allegany Mountains of Western New York, had restored my confidence a bit. "A bit." Despite the miles of hills around Cleveland and of western New York, I realized that running at three hundred feet of elevation and up to two thousand feet is not the same thing as running at nine thousand feet to 12,600 feet. In order to help acclimate to the elevation, Sue Ellen, Sean, and I went out to Colorado a week ahead of the race and spent some time running and hiking trails in Summit County and then spending three wonderful days back-packing in the high alpine region of the Holy Cross Wilderness at the headwaters of Cross Creek. Our good friend Donny Shefchik of Paragon Guides, with his assistant guide Pam, not only took us to this pristine camping site, but eased our loads by bringing three llamas to carry the bulk of supplies! It was absolutely spectacular. We even caught fish!

We came out of the backcountry on Thursday, bought supplies for the race, and tried to get a good night's sleep (it was never so good, however, as the sleep we had at eleven thousand feet while camping). Friday we explored Leadville and went to the race check-in ceremony. Let me say that I have always tried to overcome my athletic deficiencies by totally analyzing the "mechanics" of the sport; sort of a "brains over brawn" attitude. But although this helps to an extent, a bit of brawn helps too. Sue Ellen has always accused me of "over-analyzing" everything from my golf swing to my skiing to my ultra running. "Just let it happen!" And I must admit, I think she may have a point. The *anticipation* of the event is indeed thrilling and I think it is a big part of the draw; but anticipation can lead to stress as well and stress can drain the life out of the best intentions.

Leadville and the surrounding mountains, including the fourteeners of Mt. Elbert and Mt. Massive form the background of a spectacular event. There are three major climbs in this "out-and-back" course with the third climb being the longest going from the lowest point on the course (nine thousand feet at Twin Lakes) to the highest point at 12,600 feet (Hope Pass). After negotiating the final climb on the way out, the runner then turns around at Winfield (50 miles) and does it all again, in reverse.

The race started at four AM on Saturday and the first 5 or 6 miles is downhill followed by 7 or 8 miles of mostly rolling and/or flat terrain. The first "official" aid station at 13 miles should be completed well ahead of the cut-off time. I thought I was "prepared." The variable of how I would handle the altitude was still an unknown, but all in all, I was ready to do well (for me). But something strange happened to me very early. The first stage of the run did not go well for me. I felt "loopy" for reasons I still do not understand. At about the 5-mile mark, the course transitions from a smooth dirt road to a rocky road and you can guess what happened. I could not have been on the rocky road for more than ten feet before I took my first fall. Of course I opened the wounds on my knees that had only recently healed from a fall on Massanutten Mountain in May, and my hat and headlamp went sailing off and down the road as well. After scrambling about and finding my hat and headlamp, then repositioning the headlight (after a first attempt resulted in the light being upside-down), I continued to what should have been a delightful trail run around Turquoise Lake on a beautiful single-track trail. Instead, I was shaky for some reason and fell again. By the time I had gotten to the 7-mile point and the "boat ramp" where crew were allowed to visit their runner, I was surprised to find Sue Ellen ordering me on rather than having me take a break for an Ensure. I later learned that I was at the very back of the pack and needed to make up time even though I "looked terrible." Sean told Sue Ellen to "take pictures now" because he had real doubts that I would even make the next aid station!

After the first official aid station at 13 miles, things did get better. I was able to enjoy the next two climbs and the absolutely spectacular vistas they provided, as well as some sections of simply wonderful soft single-track trails circling Mt. Elbert. By the time I arrived at the 37-mile aid station at Twin Lakes (the last aid station before the climb over Hope Pass) I had nurtured a forty-five minute "cushion" over the cut-off time. I needed more. The climb from Twin Lakes to the top of Hope Pass is beautiful, but steep and long. By the time I had covered about half of the climb, I could no longer maintain any semblance of pace. I had to stop every few minutes simply to breathe! It was a "death march" to the top. The rain and hail we experienced on the way up presented no special problem (other than the time it took to take off my camelback pack, put on my raincoat, fiddle with zippers, and reposition my hydration system), but the rain had made the trail on the other side of the mountain a muddy mess. Traversing down the lower section of trail was much more like skiing than running. I had lost a lot of time. Once off the mountain and on the road to Winfield the last 3 or 4 miles to the turnaround point was a run-walk up-hill. The cut-off time was officially six PM. The station-head has the prerogative to adjust this time depending upon conditions. In this case, runners were allowed to continue up to 6:15; I arrived at 6:17.

The Leadville Trail 100 was my eighth attempt at completing a 100 miler. I have experienced being an "official" finisher twice, an "unofficial" finisher once (nine minutes over the thirty-hour cut-off), and a DNF, now five times. And I can relate that a DNF resulting from injury can be a blessing, but a DNF from simply missing a time cut-off and not injury or physical illness is a *very* empty feeling. It is the pits.

Sean went on to pace Keith Knipling. Sue Ellen and Tom took me "home." We got some sleep and awoke early to go to the finish line to cheer for the "finishers." We were happy to see the Virginia Happy Trails runners finish and especially the Knippling's, Gary and Keith, who are on their way to becoming the first father-son team to complete the Grand Slam of ultra running! It was great to see, but I must be honest, I wished that I had been one of those tired runners making their way up the final climb to the finish line at sixth and Main.

So what was my take on this event? It was great; a wonderful experience in some of the most beautiful scenery anywhere in the USA! The aid stations were great; the people were kind and always helpful. The course was incredibly well marked, making it practically impossible to get lost. And the community of Leadville, I think, is precious. I suppose the old saying about a glass being either half empty, or half full, can apply to my experience at the LT 100. And yes, absolutely, my glass was way over half full!

Jack Andrish
August 21, 2006

An Ultra Marathoner's Journey

We gathered at the start of the Leadville Trail 100 at 4:00 AM

One must be comfortable being alone with our thoughts.

Will I ever get off this mountain?

2007

The attraction of running trails and the dreams of finishing another mountain ultra do not die easily.

THE PURSUIT OF HAPPINESS

It's nearly one week since I got to the starting line of the thirteenth Massanutten Mountain Trail 100. Our plane is traveling at thirty-five thousand feet over the Atlantic Ocean and a movie is playing, *The Pursuit of Happiness*. The pursuit of happiness, that's it! Ultra running is all about the pursuit of happiness. It is all about the *pursuit*.

Last year was my first attempt to complete the MMT 100. I knew from my son and his friends that this was a very difficult course; difficult and perhaps dangerous even, with rocks and roots (especially rocks) galore. But I had crewed a couple of times for Sean and couldn't resist the chance to do it myself. After all, I was not getting any younger and my opportunities were obviously becoming limited. So under perfect weather conditions, I ran and completed all but the last 3 miles! My back had literally collapsed and I bailed at Elizabeth Furnace with only 3-plus miles to go. But I had surprised myself by almost completing the course and this year I would finish the job. I brought an assortment of back braces and I would see the last 3 miles of the MMT 100.

Cleveland had a strange winter this year; almost spring-like during December and January and then *bam!* February, March, and into April the snow came and stayed. Even Easter day brought two and a half feet of new snow.

These are not the best conditions to train on the trails through the Metro Parks of Cleveland. But I did manage a 50K in March (Arizona); a 50 mile in Virginia (BRR); and a 24-hour Adventure Run with Sue Ellen outside of DC in April. I thought that this should have toughened me up a bit for MMT. After all, I only needed 3 more miles.

Once again, this year brought perfect weather. We were so lucky. The rain on Friday opened to a clear and cool day on Saturday. The course would be a little different this year, however. Last year there were last minute changes that had to be made because of a fire at the south end of the course. Some road sections were substituted for traditional trails. And this year we would also experience traveling down "waterfall" trail as well as two trips up and over "jawbone." Oh well, what difference would that really make to the overall 100 miles? Oh was I naive!

As usual, getting to the starting line was a thrill. Sue Ellen would crew for me and Steve Core would be my pacer. Life was good. I ran the first 20-plus miles with John Nelson (or rather John ran with me since he is much faster than I am, but he had made a conscious decision to run slow in the beginning and save something for later). I did notice that some of the early climbs, such as the one after Habron Gap (24 miles), seemed longer this year (they weren't, it was just my perception). But then we moved through sections that were different from last year, such as the up-and-over section to Gap Creek 1 (39 miles) and Jawbone 1 on the way to Kerns Mountain. No road sections this year; just relentless uphills and steep downhills. And then there was "waterfall." Wow! I had only fallen once up to that section. Perhaps about mile 30 I had tripped and as my fall was imminent, I grabbed for a small tree with my right hand (I didn't want to fall on my right rib cage, still smarting from a fall a couple of weeks earlier) but this merely resulted in flinging my body 180 degrees around and landing my left thigh directly onto a rock. Ouch! But this was nothing compared to what could have been on "waterfall." About a third of the way down this very steep and rocky path, I tripped again. Oh no! As I lurched forward toward a very rocky face-first landing, I panicked. But sometimes a little adrenalin is a good thing and my feet recovered with a cat-like quickness that they had not seen for decades. I recovered and felt blessed!

The next section of the "race" is always my favorite, regardless of the event. It is the "mystical" time when day turns into night. But this year, for me, on Massanutten Mountain, this coincided with the 5-mile climb up to Bird Knob (53 miles), only to then turn around and traverse down the steep, boulder ridden top section and on again to the Rt 211 aid station (58 miles). I was fatiguing. But I had company again with my pacer and Steve was great; patient and thoughtful. Sue Ellen had met me at every available aid station and picked up my spirits (and made me drink my Ensure!). As we left 211 we moved on to Gap Creek 2. This section is claimed to be only 6.8 miles, but for me it seemed to never end. It was nice to pass the "waterfall" trail section and not have to climb up that very steep trail, but as it turned out, I may have preferred that to what we had instead; a relentless long uphill followed by a shoe-sucking mud/rock downhill. My quads were shot. I could not run a step of the downhill. And yes, I missed the time cut-off at Gap Creek 2; about 65 miles into the run and a little after 2:30 in the morning. Massanutten had won. As Sue Ellen drove me back to the start/finish, I learned that Sean had his ups and downs too, but had finished and placed fourth. And later that afternoon, I watched John Nelson finish his first 100 miler in an excellent time of just under thirty-two hours.

So why another DNF for me at a 100 miler? It has been two years and three 100 milers later since I have completed the distance. I tend to be mechanical in my analysis of problems. Heck, I'm mechanical in my approach to sports. I have always figured if I understood the mechanics well, I could achieve some level of success. And ultra running has its mechanical side in training as well as execution. I clearly was not prepared for this year's MMT; last year's MMT maybe with some forgiving road sections. But I was not for this year's course with its relentless uphills and steep downhills. I clearly had not paid my dues this winter/spring to prepare for this. But somewhere there is also a little voice in me that questions my mental toughness that is required to push through the tough times after 60 miles. I prefer not to listen to this voice, just as I prefer not to look at my (old, bent) shadow, but it's there, nonetheless.

So what *is* the attraction that brings us back? What is the attraction "that allows a man to practice a sport without ever having any hope of doing it well?" I think it is "the pursuit of happiness." And there are as many opportunities for happiness preparing for and competing in an ultra running event as there are runners in the event. Sure, it is the pure joy of crossing the finish line after successfully completing 100 miles. But it is also the happiness of merely making it to the starting line, the thrill of the first climb, the exhilaration of meeting family and friends at the first aid station and all that follow. The joy of bonding with nature while running, alone, through some backcountry trails and knowing that you are (still) "in control." It is the *pursuit* that brings us back. It is the *pursuit* that makes this dance so very difficult to let go.

I was fortunate to have had this opportunity again, to share a weekend with family and friends, participating in a wonderfully supported event, over spectacular scenery and terrain. It was a truly happy pursuit.

Jack Andrish
May 25, 2007

Why Not Golf?

Golf is nice. We get to wear comfortable clothes, walk or ride around beautifully landscaped terrain, act civil to our friends, and reminisce about our game after only a mere four or five hours of participation. I actually used to be quite good at golf. I was on our college golf team and competed in the all-Navy golf tournament during my tour of duty. In fact, for most of my adult life while playing golf, I carried a single digit handicap. So why have I turned my back on a sport that I enjoyed and did well to pursue dreams of finishing 100 miles of trail running over rocky, rooty, and mountainous terrain? Why?!

> *"A man must love a thing very much if he not only practices it without any hope of fame and money, but even practices it without any hope of doing it well."*
>
> (G. K. Chesterton)

I was never good at running. As a kid, I did have some success with sports that involved eye-hand coordination and/or "smarts;" football as a quarterback; basketball as a point guard; and baseball as a catcher. But in track, I found absolutely no success; zero, nothing, nada! And this was not for the lack of trying. I probably worked harder to find something in track that I could do, than any of the other sports where I had some talent. I was just slow, slow, slow! And no element of practice helped. But I kept trying until I finally capitulated to golf.

I suppose that my life has cycled back to the dreams of my youth. I just know that if I try harder and practice harder and smarter, that I can run faster. I just know it!

So here goes, another rhapsody to failure. Leadville Trail 100 Run, '07, was the twenty-fifth anniversary of the event. I had tried last year to complete this event and succeeded only in crossing Hope Pass, once (50 miles). The dreaded time cut-off got me. But the course was beautiful and the organizers and volunteers were great, so how could I not try again this year. But this year I would not be naive about the course and what it takes to make three major climbs, at altitude, over the first 50 miles and then turn around and do it all again, in reverse. I would train harder and smarter.

My "season" started well with good experiences at Crown King in Arizona (completing the race with my wife); Bull Run Run where Sean paced me and then a twenty-four hour Virginia run with both Sean and Sue Ellen. Life was good and my dreams of completing both Massanutten Mt. Trail 100 and Leadville were flourishing. And then came MMT and "the pursuit of happiness" which ended in a slog at 65 miles. Nonetheless, with the support of Sue Ellen, I pushed on this summer with the real intent and expectation of finishing the Leadville 100. From reading I knew that working at altitudes above eight to ten thousand feet subtracts about fifteen percent of our aerobic work capacity if we live and train (in Ohio). And for me that is a formidable statistic. Regardless of the event, even at sea level, I am always "on the bubble" when trying to meet aid station cut-off times. Subtract fifteen percent of my work capacity and the result is obvious. One solution to this handicap is to live and train at altitude for at least three to four weeks prior to the event. But since I still have a "day job," this was not an option.

Sue Ellen sent me to the Leadville Training Camp as a Father's Day gift. This was great as it gave me a chance to run the course in sections and gain familiarity. It also gave me a chance to learn from experienced Leadville finishers some valuable tips and "pearls." But I still had that fifteen percent rule to deal with. My colleagues offered to help with blood doping; but no, ultra runners, like golfers, do have personal ethics. Another offered to give me "epo," (erythropoietin) but again, the ethic thing got in the way (and besides, it would probably just make my blood thick enough to give me a stroke at altitude!). But I did get the brilliant idea that if I made myself fifteen percent heavier for my training, then when I got to Hope Pass and was fifteen percent lighter than my training weight, the two would cancel out. Perfect!

I had been preparing well this summer and then two weeks before Leadville, I decided to have one more hard work-out. I did a series of hill repeats with weights strapped to my ankles and waist and I went until I could not do more, and then did more! I thought this would provide the final "toughening" required to get me up and over Hope Pass and back again. The problem was that I tore a calf muscle in the process (medial head of the gastrocnemius) and acutely developed a very swollen and painful leg. It of course brought my running to an immediate stop, and I then depended upon an elastic stocking, Motrin, and my intrinsic healing ability to overcome this; in two weeks! It showed promise after about ten days, but at the Friday pre-race check-in it began swelling again and was quite sore; and I was limping. I did find an elastic sleeve in a pharmacy that fit tightly around my leg and it felt pretty good with that. And that is how I started the race; with my right leg bound by an elastic brace applied tightly over a TED elastic support hose and of course the "special" back brace I had found last year in the Co-op Feed Store in Middlefield. With all of this I actually felt good at the start. But I just couldn't muster up much speed and then, while circling Mt. Elbert at around 10,500-plus feet, I developed a bit of high-altitude pulmonary edema and just couldn't make the time cut-off at Twin Lakes (40 miles). And oh yes, while working through my breathing difficulties I was also dodging lightning bolts for about an hour and a half (not my favorite pastime).

I must admit that as I was descending from the Mt. Elbert section to my final aid station, the thought of being a golfer once again seemed like a good idea. But given a day or two of (mental) recovery, I realized that as long as I am able, I can't give up on the feeling that if I train harder and smarter, I just know I can get up and over Hope Pass and back again! I just know it.

Jack Andrish
August 27, 2007

2008

Why Jack! Why carry on in this fashion? I have heard that the definition of insanity is doing something over and over again and expecting a different outcome. I don't know if that is actually a correct definition, but I think that many of my friends back home had their suspicions.

Call Me Ishmael and The "Beeg Fish"

I remember many years ago watching Spencer Tracy play an old man who took his fishing boat out to sea every day, in search of the "beeg fish." He had nothing but respect for his adversary for it was his world that the old man was entering and in his world, the "beeg fish" was king. Every day he would plan a new strategy and every day he would imagine just what he would do with such a catch. But then, the old man would return from the sea every day with thanksgiving for whatever he had caught; but never the "beeg fish." Then one day in his small boat, he did the unimaginable. He caught the "beeg fish!" He caught the beautiful, powerful master of the sea. Of course, from then on, the epic struggle of the old man and the sea played out. The old man survived, the "beeg fish" did not and by the time the boat finally made it home, the "beeg fish" had been eaten by prey. The epic struggle of man against the sea ended with a hollow victory for the old man and a reaffirmation of the natural power and majesty of the sea.

I may not have everything correct here in this recollection. Forgive me for, after all, it was probably forty plus years ago that I saw the movie and/or read the book. But as I circled Mt. Elbert for the third time in the past three years, I felt for the old man. The Leadville Trail 100 has become my "beeg fish." A search, but not a catch.

Off and on for the past twenty years I and my family have played in the wintertime in the mountains that look over Leadville as we do our yearly "hut skiing." It seemed reasonable to set a goal of completing the LT 100 as an excuse to play in the same mountains in the summer. My first attempt was in 2006. That year I felt "loopy" for the first 13 miles, fell a couple of times early, and struggled up and over Hope Pass, only to miss the time cut-off at the 50 mile turn around at Winfield. The next year I was intent to beat myself up during training. My theory was to run with twenty pounds of lead weight around my ankles and waist as I trained in Cleveland so that when I would run at altitude without the extra weight, it all would somehow even out. All that led to was a ruptured calf muscle two weeks before the race and another DNF; this time at the Twin Lakes 40 mile mark.

This year was to be "my time." I would not over train. I would not go into Leadville hurt or "loopy." I would run a smart race, and finish! Granted, I recognized that some odds were against me. For whatever reason, my times over the past year in 50 milers have been significantly slower than ever before. And I recognized that Gary Knipling, who is *at least* three hours faster than me over 50 miles and the same age as I am, finished Leadville last year as part of the Grand Slam, but with only thirty minutes to spare. And my friend Tom Bauer, who ran a 50 miler this spring in Arizona, five hours faster than me, finished Leadville last year in twenty-eight hours. I recognize totally that the thirty-hour limit is/would/will be a tough "beeg fish" to catch.

The weather in Leadville this year was interesting. I have come to realize and accept that dodging lightning bolts from the obligatory afternoon and evening thunderstorms is par for this course. But this year, the lightning was interspersed among rain, hail, and snow with temperatures that ranged from the thirties to moments of fifties. It was a cold and wet experience. The first 13 miles of the LT 100 are a really nice "warm up." Perhaps the first third of that section is downhill on mostly dirt road. The rest of the first section is a beautiful trip around Turquoise Lake on gentle single-track trail. I arrived at the 13-mile aid station about twenty minutes ahead of the cut-off. This was about what I expected. The next section traverses back through a beautiful forest (I know, I use that word "beautiful" a lot; but it fits), makes a short climb, and then emerges upon the Hagerman Pass Road. This is a long, gentle climb with spectacular views of Turquoise Lake below and Hagerman Pass above. The course eventually diverts back up and over Sugarloaf Mountain only to descend down to the Fish Hatchery aid station. I wasn't struggling (I thought) but I only made the cut-off by one minute! I was shocked and surprised to be in such a bind at only a marathon distance. The next 5-mile section should be run since it is a flat road and then at least partly runnable for another 3 miles as it is a gentle uphill and on dirt road. But my breathing was labored and my leg speed was non-existent. Oh my, with fifteen minutes to go until the next aid station cut-off I was told by a volunteer walking down the road that I could only make the cut-off if I "basically ran" the whole way. Well, gasping and groping, I ran (mostly) and I did make the cut-off, again by one minute! But that allowed me to make the climb up to Mt. Elbert and traverse the beautiful single-track trail (yes, there's that word again) that winds around Elbert and then eventually descends to Twin Lakes (40 miles). It was within this section that I succumbed to the reality of my inadequacy. It was within this section that I began remembering the suffering of the old man and the sea and his quest to capture the "beeg fish." And yes, I failed by a long shot to make the Twin Lakes time cut-off. I'm now three for three in Leadville Trail 100 DNFs.

As I was engaged in my last section of the race, my mind told me "That's enough!" I'm not going to put myself and my family through this exercise in "failure" again. But disappointment and anger soon turned to frustration. Yes, frustration. I just know that I can catch this "beeg fish!" I only have to train smarter and yes, to live at altitude for at least a month before the race. Perhaps retirement may have its benefits?

And oh yes, I know that "Ishmael" was part of a chase of another kind of "monster" of the sea and from another book; but somehow, I just felt like the name fit my story.

Jack Andrish
August 20, 2008

> Life isn't about waiting for the storm to pass . . .
> It's about learning to dance in the rain.
> (unknown, 2008)

2009

Tell me that I am not alone. I was fortunate enough to be accepted to the Western States 100 for the fifth time (unheard of now with the lottery giving the average runner a less than ten percent chance of acceptance). I had been on schedule with my training that winter and then, one week before I was to run the Old Pueblo 50 Mile ultra outside of Tucson, I stepped out of my car after an easy run and my right knee "exploded" in pain. Now pain is no stranger to an ultra runner and the psyche of our tribe is self-reliance and the ability to overcome. "Pain is inevitable but suffering is optional." "Pain is weakness leaving the body." These are common mantras to the ultra runner. And so, when I stepped out of my car and had this explosive pain in my knee, I denied the importance. Resting over-night, the next morning I tried to test it out with an easy run. "Good try, Jack." I could not ignore my injury this time. I limped and hobbled for a couple of miles, only to make my knee swell like a cantaloupe. Okay, I now had only three months before what would surely be my last tango in the Sierra Nevada mountains on the Western States Trail. Only three months! I had to cancel my entry into the Old Pueblo 50-mile run. I enlisted one of my colleagues to help me get an MRI (which showed a displaced tear of the medial meniscus as well as injury to the articular surface) and then to urgently have a knee arthroscopy with debridement of "stuff." The following "diary" reflects my somewhat frantic efforts to recover and "train" for my forthcoming Western States 100. I suspect that I am not the only runner who has traveled this road; in fact, as an orthopaedic surgeon myself, I realize that my experience is shared by many.

Diary of a Recovery

February 28, 2009:
Went for an "easy" 11 mile run in preparation for Old Pueblo. It was cold. I wore my old trail shoes. Whatever cushion they once had was long gone. The run was purposefully at a slow pace (don't want to get hurt before OP). No problems until I got home and got out of the car. Oops! Pain! Different kind of knee pain. Followed by swelling.

March 1, 2009:
Sunday morning. Let's try to see what I can do. Most of these things we can run through. But not this. One mile only and that was with significant pain and limp. This is different.

March 2, 2009:
MRI. Torn medial meniscus and some articular cartilage damage. Acute chondral (cartilage) fracture? Let's just take charge and scope the knee. This will mean no Old Pueblo 50 Mile; but the bigger picture is Western States and that is only three and a half months away.

March 5, 2009:
Surgery. No surprises (unfortunately); torn meniscus, but full thickness loss of articular cartilage on medial femoral condyle. Arthritis!

March 9, 2009:
Back to work. Two cases in the morning and clinic in the afternoon.

March 14, 2009:
Went for a 1 mile walk in the Metro Park. Didn't feel too bad and even "ran" a few steps. No problem. There's hope.

March 16, 2009:
Okay. Time to start a regular exercise program at the gym. Light PREs (Progressive Resistance Exercises) and stationary bike, just for motion. No problem.

March 20, 2009:
Walked a fairly long distance (one half mile) from Education Building to Anatomy Lab, with heavy briefcase. Knee starts to hurt a bit.

March 23, 2009:
Knee hurts more. Limp. Going to gym and those workouts okay, but limp (and pain) walking.

April 1, 2009:
Drove to North Carolina with family to support Sue Ellen's effort for the Umstead 100 Mile Endurance Run. More pain and more limp.

April 4, 2009:
Sue Ellen is doing great!! Walked a 12.5 mile loop with her. Tried to run, but couldn't, too much pain. Walked the whole thing, but with limp and pain (this was her fifth loop and she was more than willing to walk at this point).

April 6, 2009:
Continue with the gym workouts. Going well and able to elevate my heart rate on stationary bike. Continued to increase aerobics to forty-fifty-sixty minutes.

April 18, 2009:
Okay, time to try to run! But I soon find I can't. Pain prohibits. I try to run/walk but I can't run. Finally I try to see if I can slow down to a crawl with less pain and it works. I do the run/walk thing but with the "run" averaging twenty-four and a half minutes per mile! But by the end of the 3-mile effort, I could extend the "run" with little pain. Hope!

April 19, 2009:
Let's see if it works two days in a row; it doesn't. I can sustain this agonal pace, but only with pain and only at a nearly twenty-five minute/mile pace.

I really can't see how I can come from this to run the WS Training Camp in one month. Western States is looking doubtful. But my plan will be to try to run at whatever pace I can do, four to five times a week and to continue to go to the gym twice a week for weight training and once a week for an intense aerobic workout on the bike. That is my plan!

April 23, 2009:
It's not going to happen.

April 28, 2009:
This is driving me crazy. I take ibuprofen and the knee feels "almost" like normal, with walking. I think I can run. I do run but within a few yards the (medial) knee pain returns. I limp. I can only shuffle although a week ago I could only shuffle at most a quarter mile without stopping and last night I could shuffle 1.5 miles at a time (four total). But it is a painful shuffle and not enough to get me to the first aid station in time. I don't think I will be able to participate in the training camp; and very doubtful for WS a month later. I may try a knee injection. And although I don't want to, I may try an unloader brace (I'm still convinced that the pain is not from the chondral loss, but from some synovial irritation). Am I in denial?

April 29, 2009:
Broke down and got an "unloader" brace. It didn't feel like it was doing much, but I tried it out on a trail and for the first time since surgery, I ran! Not a shuffle; for the most part I could get both feet off the ground at the same time. Total mileage, only 3 miles, but 2.5 miles were running. The brace knocked the pain level from an eight to a five, maybe even a four. And there were moments when my pace was sub-ten minute mile. Overall, the running pace was below a fourteen minute/mile and that is a ten minute/mile faster than I could do ten days ago! Is there hope? If I can do this for 3 miles, can I do it for 30 miles; for 50 miles; for 100 miles?

April 30, 2009:
Pain and swelling. Limp. Downer!

May 1, 2009:

Feeling better. Can walk with little limp and just some soreness. I can deal with this if this is as bad as it gets following a run. But can I run more than a couple of miles? It is still such a long way to go.

May 8, 2009:

Up and down. At a meeting in South Carolina. Found a National Forest with a beautiful trail to run. I ran and for the first time there was no real pain with running! A bit sore, but not a limitation. The limitation is still just the extreme effort required to drag my recovering leg around; the pace is still very slow. But it was my first "official" trail run in the past two and a half months; I got dirty and I tripped over a root and fell and skinned my knee; great! But that was yesterday and today—limp and soreness.

May 9, 2009:

Ran 2.5 miles (half up a long hill and half down). The good news is that I did it at almost my "normal" pace. The bad news is that it hurt all the way. I don't know how I can carry a pace over any significant distance. I'm not even close.

I did get to the starting line that year, but to no surprise, I could not maintain a sufficient pace and was timed out at 27 miles.

2011

Time passes, but not the dreams. When will we compromise on our dreams? What will it take?

When Did it Happen?

Well, it has been four years since my last race report, five years since I finished all but the last 3 miles of "Massanutten," and seven years since my last "official" 100-mile finish. Perhaps it is time for another report. I used to enjoy the recall of another 100-mile attempt by putting pen to paper with emotions laid bare. I enjoyed sharing the experience. But then as my DNFs mounted and my performances became more lame, I lost the thrill of the recall and became somewhat embarrassed to share my experience. Why did it happen?

Ultra running and especially trail ultras continue to capture me. The opportunity for the shared participations of the runners, the crews and the pacers with events that push the limits of human endurance, is mystical. The opportunities to unite families in such a special way is precious. No wonder this dance is so difficult to forfeit. But is there a need to release from the dream?

The year 2006 was pivotal for me. I was prepared for MMT and for most of it I was having the best 100 miler of my life. But then the "wheels came off," so they say, and the last 20 miles were a struggle. Yes, my back gave out and I was a rumpled mess coming into Elizabeth Furnace. I dropped with only 3 miles to go. I had known that I had "slight" scoliosis, but I had no idea just how bad it had progressed in recent years. I got home and had an x-ray which (as a scoliosis surgeon myself) frankly scared me. It scared me not so much for the possibilities of progressive deformity and maybe surgery, but for the thought that this might be the thing that would stop me from participating in those mystical experiences I had come to love. Yes, I was panicked and proceeded to work through any number of back braces that might allow me to continue to run. And I finally did find one; not the expensive spinal orthotics I tried from our orthotics section of the Cleveland Clinic, but a $12 elastic back support I found on sale (for $8) at the feed store I use for my barn animals. It took a bit of getting used to because it squeezes the abdomen so much that diaphragmatic breathing is all but nil. On the other hand, it helped to keep my ribs off my pelvis and somewhat stabilized my core. So "deal with it" and move on!

I then entered a three-year cycle of attempting to complete the Leadville 100. The Leadville area is special to my family because of its proximity to the tenth Mountain Hut and Trail System we have used every year for the past twenty years for our backcountry skiing adventures. But I could never get beyond the turnaround at 50 miles. And then I also noticed after attending one of the LT 100 Training Camps, that even with fresh legs, I was barely making the projected time cut-offs. Oh, it must be the altitude! But then, for my last attempt at Leadville I decided to train at home by wearing twenty pounds of weights around my ankles and doing hill repeats. Oh yes, that would do it; wrong! That only made my right knee swell like a bowling ball with pain that made it difficult to walk well, less say run. Interesting, "must be a bursa." (Ignorance and Denial)

Then came 2009. I had made the Western States Lottery and had a great "game plan" for my training. The first "training" race on my agenda was the Old Pueblo 50 miler. The weekend before the race I went for an "easy" 11 miler but when I got home my right knee was swelling like a balloon and very painful. I tried to run the next day, but could barely walk. Panicked, I got an MRI on Monday, found torn meniscus, had surgery on Thursday (found torn meniscus, and arthritis), and spent the next fourteen months painfully limping threw a series of unloader braces and miserable race attempts. And then, one year ago, a physical therapist friend of mine from Australia (Jenny McConnell) taught me a method of taping for "synovial fat pad impingement" and by some miracle, no pain! I could run without a knee brace. I could run! (Oh yes, I still need the back brace. I'm afraid I'm stuck with that one.) And so the dream survives! Bring on Massanutten and those last 3 miles!

What a great spring this has been with the anticipation of MMT. Yes, training in Cleveland is problematic, but taking two weekends to visit Sean in Leesburg and training on parts of the MMT course was great. There was just one small wrinkle to my visits to Massanutten. Even with fresh legs, my times on parts of the course were just on the bubble of projected cut-off times for MMT; visions of Leadville! But the thrill of being a participant was once again precious. Certainly a year ago I had doubts of even running at all without pain and a brace. So this is truly a gift I have received and I understand that. To be there at all is a gift. I did not publicize my 2011 intentions to my friends. I was going to run MMT and finish and then share the experience. But this year my performance reflected my "diminishing skills." Despite the support from Sue Ellen and the anticipation of Sean being my pacer, my times at each aid station were just "on the bubble." I had no cushion at all. I was running and I was thrilled to be intimidated by "all those rocks!" But I could only muster bubbles. The climb out of Elizabeth Furnace did me in. I was not at all metabolically nor physically trashed; just not enough stamina to climb at the necessary pace to keep me legal. I missed my time cut-off at Shawl Gap (mile 37.6). I had to turn in my number and go home.

So what is the message? As I ran in to my final aid station, the captain congratulated me for making it this far and then told me, "Jack, there are easier hundreds out there." Yes, others have been telling me that as well. "There are easier hundreds out there." But we know it is not just about the miles! It is not just about running 100 miles. It is about overcoming fears and obstacles and achieving our dreams. It is about the dreams! As I sit here in a coffee house in Leesburg, there are still runners chasing that dream. There are still runners crossing that final grassy meadow to the finish line of the MMT 100. There are still runners. I should be there with them. I should. I still have two legs and a heart at least at this point that can withstand the effort; the effort to train and to finish. Age is relative and I'm not about to use that excuse. Not yet. Yes, there are other hundreds out there. And there are 50 milers and 50Ks that are special opportunities to share. There are! But then again, there is the mountain.

Jack Andrish
May 15, 2011

Addendum

Oh yes; it wasn't a quarter mile onto Short Mountain when I tripped and fell, face-first on one of those infamous Massanutten rocks! A little blood completes the picture.

And then, as I was coming into the final part of the trail to Shawl Gap, I encountered a very big rattlesnake! At first, I thought the sound was coming from some insect. But I looked up just in time to see the snake about three feet away. I stopped. It moved to the side of the trail and coiled. I mistakenly thought that when it coiled up, that it was resting and would be quiet. Still, we continued to look at each other for what seemed like a long time and I was debating whether to just walk on by, or walk around. Fortunately, I decided not to trust him and I bushwhacked through the opposite side of the trail. I should have known, but later learned that when a rattlesnake coils, it means he is readying himself to strike!

2012

Ultra Running, Strange Sport

Ultra running is surely bipolar. We all experience at some time (sometimes more in some of us than others) the realization that we have gone as far as we can with our (limited) skills and that we will now enjoy the 4 miler and a good golf game. Absolutely. Non-negotiable. We have learned our lesson and will now justifiably move on with our lives. We will be grateful for what we have been able to do in this sport and realize an honorable end. Yes! The revelation usually comes somewhere between half to three fourths of the way through (another) unsuccessful (DNF) ultra. Yes! How long can the DNFs go on? When will the inevitable be recognized and accepted? When will it be okay to accept our limitations?

Beats me! I'm now sixty-eight and in the best of times, my ultra finishes were the result of very hard work and still finishing in the very back of the pack. My last "official" finishes were at age sixty with WS and Wasatch. The next year I finished WS, but nine minutes over the thirty-hour limit. The next year I got to 97 miles at Massanutten and recognized, for the first time, the impact of a collapsing scoliotic spine. No more (official) 100-mile finishes. None for the past eight years. Three years ago my knee kicked back requiring surgery and the recognition of "arthritis." I have been able to complete some 50Ks and even 50 miles, but slowly. But no 100 milers.

And so it was yesterday that I DNFed for the third time, our local Burning River 100 Mile Endurance Run. The conditions were as good as it gets for

Cleveland in the mid-summer. But the really severe cramping in my legs and thigh eventually brought me to a stop at mile 46.5. Funny thing, that is exactly what happened to me last year and is the only race where I have had trouble with cramping; none with Promise Land and none with Laurel Highlands. Funny! Strange! And yes, I took enough salt and fluids (and not too much aka: Tim Noakes, author of *Waterlogged*). But I FINALLY realized my limits and realized that I was thankful for the time I have had with ultras and now I will be happy with regular runs of 4 and 5 miles and maybe the occasional 50K. Yep. I finally came to grips with time and age and the "stuff" that accompanies both. That is actually a "freeing" epiphany. Time to move on, no conflicts with job and home, time to finally work on my golf game. Freeing! I slept well.

But then came the day after. Ah, the "day after" an ultra DNF. Disappointing, but now comes (again), hope. Hope and the "recognition" that I think I have figured out the reason for my last two DNFs; the leg cramps. I really don't enjoy extended running on level surfaces. I enjoy the physicality of the variable running and walking dictated by the hills and variable terrain of trail ultras. I actually enjoyed the push up Apple Orchard Falls at Promise Land. Yep. But I hate the long flat stretches of JFK and the long runs on our own Tow Path that parallels the Ohio Canal. And so, my long "runs" are really run/walk "runs" within our hilly Metro Park system. But the Burning River 100 has lots of extended running. In fact, the first 20-plus miles are all about "running." So now I know the "why" of my DNFs. I understand. Just maybe if I train differently (and work on CORE strengthening), just maybe I can still do it. Actually, not just "maybe," but I really know with the proper preparation (and a little ultra-luck with the weather and with injury), I can do it! And as for my golf game, well that's always an option, should I ever truly realize that it is time to "move on."

Ultra running, strange sport.

Jack Andrish
July 29, 2012

The miles take their toll.

2015

THE DARK SIDE OF THE MOUNTAIN

It has been several years since I wrote a "race report." And those "reports" were always following my efforts at the 100-mile variety. I would pour my emotions into those sometimes successful and often not successful, but always "mystical" experiences. But stuff happens when one translates from sixty to seventy and this back-of-the-pack runner has had increasing problems with making time cut-offs. So it is that my resurrection of a race report comes after running a mere 13.5 miles.

The Promise Land 50K Ultra is truly one of the Virginia ultra running gems. Nestled in the Blue Ridge Mountains and not far from Lynchburg, it sports somewhere between seven to eight thousand feet of elevation gain spread over 34.5 miles (those are Horton miles, which means the stated milage is typically an underestimate of the actual milage), with Nature's beauty everywhere; up, down, and sideways. My son, Sean, had always told me that if I were to ever run one of the Horton races, Promise Land should be the one. And so in 2012, Sean and I ran together. And as happens, that year what started out in beautiful weather, suddenly turned very foul with a nearly twenty-degree drop in temperature and a deluge of rain, thunder, and the dreaded lightning. That year there was only one time cut-off at mile 23.9 and we made that time, but finished the race about ten minutes over the ten-hour time limit. Still, we finished and I was happy to have made it up the Apple Orchard Falls, back through Sunset Fields and down to the finish. The next year, 2013, I came back with my daughter Shannon, and we ran together. That year, however, a soft time cut-off had been added at the first encounter with the Sunset Fields aid station, mile 11.94 (aka 13.5) with the "suggestion" to consider dropping if one exceeded 9:15 AM. We made both cut-offs and together we experienced the ups and downs of an ultra and both finished in "official" times. And then last year I came back to participate in another Promise Land 50K, although I was hampered by multiple myofascial pains, the most problematic being a pain in the butt, and all secondary to the initiation of statin medication for control of cholesterol. Eventually, I discontinued this masochistic therapy and the pains have, as expected, ceased to exist. That said, it hobbled me last year and for the first time at the 50K level, I missed a time cut-off (Sunset Fields) by a lot!

So this past year I have ceased the statins (while initiating a "secondary" cholesterol lowering drug and promising to pay more attention to diet) and returned to running as time has allowed. It has been good to run again with only the "usual" aches and pains of adulthood. My plan was to return to the Promise Land 50K, but only if I could demonstrate to myself that I could at least make the first time cut-off at Sunset Fields. I would make a special trip to Virginia in March and run the first part of the course. If I could make it within the allotted time frame, I would send in my entry form and register. If I couldn't make it, then I would accept that it was now beyond my capability. And so, Sue Ellen and I made the drive. On a March Saturday morning she left me at the Promise Land Camp and waved to me as I started my "run" up and over and around Onion Mountain and then down to Sunset Fields where she was there to time me. I made what I thought was within one minute of the time cut-off (9:15 AM, 3:45 into the race), but I had struggled up the final climb onto the Parkway crossing. That said, I thought that was good enough to go back and "train" and prepare for the race. I made out an official entry.

David Horton often has a way with words and his description of the course beyond the first encounter with Sunset Fields is "the dark side" of the mountain. And so my goal this year was to finish, but especially at least to get to the "dark side" of the mountain. I was going to the "dark side!"

But the night before the race I found a real problem. Reading the "runners' packet" I found that last year the time cut-off at Sunset Fields had been reduced to 9:05. I had been thinking of it as the 2013 time of 9:15 (and that was a "soft" time cut-off at that). Now I had to reduce my time by another ten minutes over the 13.5 miles.

The conditions for the race this year were perfect for running an ultra; cloudy, intermittent light showers, with temperatures in the forties. Perfect. My strategy was to maintain the best pace I could carry and run at every opportunity and work the uphills with a steady pace. And I did. And this time when I crossed the Parkway following the final climb, I felt good; no struggling this time. And then for the 1.7 miles downhill into Sunset Fields, I ran as fast as I could; and I could! In fact, my Garmin watch recorded a maximum speed of 9.9 mph! But as I entered the aid station, I was greeted with the dreaded "you missed the time cut-off by ten minutes" and there are no exceptions. "You are out of the race."

Now I am rather experienced at being timed out in races, but it has always been mostly a blessing because I had been struggling with the proverbial "death march." But this time I felt good; really good! I was not tired. I had no pain. I was metabolically intact. And I REALLY wanted to get to the "dark side" of the mountain. But I could not persuade. "We have observed that ten minutes over at this time in the race translates to an hour over the cut-off on the rest of the course, and no one working an aid station wants to work until four PM."

And so, Sue Ellen reluctantly drove me back to our room at the Peaks of Otter Lodge (a great location, by the way, for accommodations for this race) and after a snack, we went out together and hiked to the top of Sharp Top Mountain (the second highest peak in Virginia). All in all, it was a great day for us. But of course I was bothered by my DNF. I was disappointed not to see the "dark side" of the mountain, and confused. I was confused because I felt so good. Too good? Is it just time to forget running ultras, or at least to forget mountain ultras? After all, I am seventy-one years old and as a famous ex-quarterback of the Cleveland Browns (Bernie Kosar) found out from an ex-head football coach of the Browns (Bill Belichick), "diminishing skills" comes with age. And the sensible thing to accept is to eliminate the mountains. The relentless climbing required is not the most enjoyable thing to experience. It's tough and all too often a struggle. But then eventually the struggle does end and the other side of the mountain is downhill!

So after a good night's sleep and a drive back to Ohio with time to think, I now understand. Sure, the bad news was that I missed the time cut-off, but the good news was that I did climb the mountain and I felt good! I felt strong! I had experienced relentless climbs and some wonderful extended downhill running as well. I was so lucky and fortunate. And then I had completed the day by climbing another mountain with my wife. Nothing bad about any of that!

So what are my plans for the future? I will continue to run as long as my body and mind allow. But I will be happy with whatever pace I can put forth. And I will not necessarily do it in a "race," but I can make my own events at my pace, self-contained or otherwise. I will enjoy and be thankful for the opportunities. And I will return to Virginia in the spring and begin my "race" at the Promise Land Camp, and I will climb the mountain and I will go beyond the Sunset Fields and I will see the "dark side" of the mountain.

Jack Andrish
April 26, 2015

The joy of anticipation.

2015

THE DECISIONS WE MAKE
BOONSBORO, MD

In the spring of 1963 President John F. Kennedy, in an effort to encourage physical fitness, arranged for a series of 50 mile "challenges" around the country. Following his assassination, the "challenge" held in Washington County, Maryland became the JFK 50 Mile Memorial and has been held every November since then.

My first 50-mile event was the JFK 50 Mile ultra marathon. I was fifty-five years old and a "newbie" to running ultras. My son, Sean, while still living in Leesburg, Virginia had run his first 50 miler at the JFK 50 a couple of years before. I was amazed and fearful for him that he could have hurt himself running that far. Fifty miles! That said, since his first running of the JFK 50 I had become hooked on trail running and had even completed a 50K ultra. So in 1999 I ran my first JFK 50 and even completed it within a qualifying time for the Western States 100.

I'm not sure, no I am sure, that I never really enjoyed all 50 miles. I did enjoy the first 13-plus miles on the Appalachian Trail (AT) but after exiting the trail section, the runners entered onto an excruciating 26-mile effort on the C&O canal tow path. Flat and seemingly never ending, it was always a relief when I would exit the canal tow path and move to the final 8 miles running pastoral rolling hills on country roads onto the finish line in Williamsport, Maryland. I continued to run the JFK 50 every year for the next ten years. I ran it partly as a tradition but also as a qualifier for the Western States 100, which had now become my obsession. Unfortunately, at age sixty-five, following knee surgery and wearing a hinged brace, I failed to finish my eleventh attempt. The next year however, 2010, I ran again and finished, but not within a Western States qualifying time.

Now we fast-forward to 2015. A lot of water had passed over the dam and my realization that my ultra days were numbered prompted me to try one more time to run and complete our "traditional" JFK 50. It had been five years since I last ran it and I had forgotten. I had forgotten that I had run and completed the race following my DNF the year before; the year of my knee injury and surgery. I had forgotten and I didn't want the memory of my last JFK 50 to be a DNF. In retrospect I wish I had remembered because now in 2015 at the age of seventy-one (two-weeks shy of age seventy-two), I was lining up for my thirteenth running of the JFK 50! I was reasonably prepared and confident. But I should have been concerned when after only 3 miles of road and exiting onto the Trail, I tripped and fell over a timing mat! We should also recognize that the AT is beautiful with rolling climbs and descents, often overlooking pastures, forests, and at times the Potomac River. But it is also relentlessly filled with rocks. Yes, it is a very rocky trail. In my "youth" I enjoyed developing the skill to glide over rocky trails, but at age seventy-one that skill had been transformed into a careful "never take your eyes off the trail" pace. So following my less than graceful entry onto the Trail, I was careful but still making reasonable time. Life was good and I began to prepare for the next section along the C&O Canal tow path. It was only about 2 miles from the descent from the Trail that I took my eye off the ball (or should I say the rocky trail). I had passed most of the most technical section. I was entering a descent from the ridge over-looking the river below when it happened! I tripped on a root and pitched forward. Now in this split-second decisions are made; a split second. My first thought was that I was not going to recover from this tripping so I needed to decide the "how" I should proceed. On the right side of the trail was a small tree. Should I fall to the right and grab the tree in an effort to prevent a complete fall? Maybe, but I had been there before and remembered that flinging around a tree was tantamount to dislocating a shoulder. No, I should just accept the fall forward. Take my scrapes and bruises as I had done hundreds of times over the years and then carry on. So I did, but when I landed upon the leaf covered trail (the JFK 50 is held in November and most of the trails are still covered with fallen leaves) my left hip landed really hard. I was confused because I wasn't fully aware of what made this landing so hard. Removing a few leaves, however, gave the answer: a rock. I had landed hard against a rock onto my left hip. I must say, I did know something was wrong. I did recognize that I may have broken my hip. I couldn't move. The good news was, however, that two men were camping just above the trail and noticed me. They came to the rescue and lifted me up and sat me on a tree stump. Sitting on the stump was not painful. I tried to convince myself that it was just a bruise, but each time I tried to stand up there would be a lancinating pain that told me "No way."

Recognizing that I was not going to be able to continue, my new friends used their cell phones to call for help. A first responder team using off-road four-wheelers managed to bushwhack their way to our perch. Using the four-wheeler to get me down was interesting. They picked me up and placed me on the back seat. Holding onto the side bars which allowed me to push my butt up and off the seat, my team spent the next few hours clearing a trail down the mountain for the four-wheeler and me. All totaled, it took about five hours from the time I fell until we arrived off the mountain and into a waiting ambulance. I was taken to the hospital in Hagerstown, MD where I spent the night. The next day a team from my workplace (Cleveland Clinic) came and flew me home where the following day one of my orthopaedic colleagues "pinned" my hip.

So what is my take on my thirteenth running of the JFK 50 miler? Two decisions probably could have been better. The first decision was to run at all, forgetting that indeed I had run and completed the event five years before. The second was the split-second decision I made to not try to break my fall by grabbing that small tree by the side of the trail. Who knows if that would have avoided injury, but most likely it would have at least avoided the broken hip.

Will this C&O Canal Tow Path ever end?!

Fun on the Appalachian Trail

Working our way down Weverton Cliffs

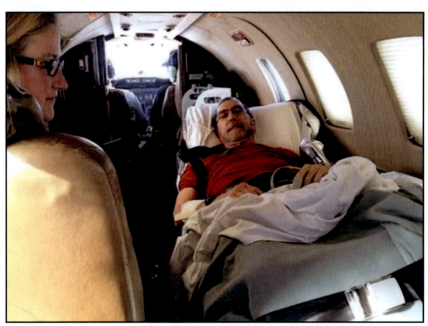
Not the way I envisioned my finish for my 13th running of the JFK 50 mile

An Ultra Marathoner's Journey

An Aid Station for All

You know it can get pretty lonely out there during an ultra marathon. In fact, to be an ultra runner, one must be comfortable being alone with their thoughts. There is great comradery among runners and crew and volunteers, but as the miles become endless miles and the footsteps become solitary footsteps, the expectation of arriving at an aid station can be as illusional as an oasis. In fact, the aid station is an oasis of sorts. They appear anywhere from 3 to 25 miles apart into the race and provide the opportunity to refuel and rehydrate. In fact, many of the aid stations provide a smorgasbord of food ranging from "junk" to bananas, oranges, and watermelon. And especially for aid stations later in the race, there can be soup and Ramon noodles! In addition to nutritional "aid," they can cover first aid requirements and personal hygiene supplies. For a few of the selected aid stations, there can be an opportunity to meet with your support system, your "crew" as well. And we should also know that the term "crew" stands for "Cranky Runner Endless Waiting." So true! And then there is "the chair." Another ultra mantra is "beware of the chair!" Empathetic family and/or aid station volunteers may offer a chair to sit down on, but the temptation to remain in the chair often takes a bit of "tough love" to get the runner up and running again. That said, any runner will tell you that the support received by the volunteers (and family) at these aid stations is critical to having a successful experience. Whether a runner or a volunteer, ultras are truly family affairs.

Now I should also point out that the numbers of ultras in the Cleveland, Ohio area are plentiful. The "Emerald Neckless" of metro parks surrounding Cleveland is a treasure. Add to that the Cuyahoga Valley National Park system, and you have the basis for hundreds of miles of trails to run. In 2007, the first running of the Burning River 100 Mile Endurance Run was held. It stretched from the east side of Cleveland in a metro park and extended south through adjoining park systems (metro and national), ending in Cuyahoga Falls. For ten years my wife and I and our family and friends managed one of the aid stations about 30 miles into the race; the Egbert Picnic Area aid station. We carried on as aid station "captains" for ten years. During that time it became a family "tradition" to organize the aid station and tend to the needs of the runners. Our two granddaughters grew up with this experience (and "tradition") as well, starting at ages two and three (watching) and eventually evolving to providing water refills and most importantly, dispensing popsicles!

Night-time aid, another kind of mystical experience

Popsicles anyone? My granddaughters as aid station workers

2016

BACKSIDE 50, BURNING RIVER 2016

Okay. Yesterday was a really great day for me. Our Egbert aid station was the best ever thanks to all of our wonderful, experienced volunteers! It was fun and I think the runners were well supported.

As for me, I tried the "Back Side 50" (the second 50 miles of the 100 mile Burning River event). With a sixteen-hour time limit, I thought this was a very doable race for me and an opportunity to finally see the "back side." But that was not the case. Once again, I could not maintain a pace to make the cut-offs and was pulled at Pine hollow, 20 miles for me. That said, I did have the "mystical experience" of running into the night! And I ran at a pace that was not threatening to me and a pace where I was not trashing my body and was able to have fun. During the night portion, I felt like I could "run" forever. I was connecting to the night-time environment and even singing to myself on the sections where I was not avoiding rocks and roots. It was great. I felt bad that my pace did not allow me to continue, but I am grateful for the opportunity to have experienced what I could. So "Thank You," Burning River Endurance Run.

And what else did I learn? I am afraid that I have finally come to terms with my "diminishing skills" and will need to pick my event participations more selectively and with forgiving terrain and time limits. The good news is that there are such events out there. So I will continue to run as long as I can, and at a pace that allows me to enjoy the experience.

2018

Déjà Vu All Over Again or Why Can't I Just Say No!

Okay. It is now 2018 and I am just shy of my seventy-fifth birthday. I have repeatedly "convinced" myself that I am no longer safe nor able to complete and participate in a timed ultra other than the twenty-four-hour run format without the pressure of time cutoffs. And yet here I was, September 30, 2018, in Brownsville, Vermont at the starting line of the Vermont 50K. Really?

A race in Vermont had always been on my bucket list of ultras. My family has a long history of playing in the mountains of Vermont. Years ago I even signed up for the 100 mile version, but had to drop out because of a work conflict. As time passed and my running skills diminished, participating in a Vermont ultra dropped from my thoughts until a few years ago when I came back to Vermont to crew for my son, running the Vermont 100-mile endurance run. It was beautiful. I was hooked once more. I had to come back and bring my wife, Sue Ellen, to share the revival of memories long-past from our many family vacations. And what better "excuse" than to sign up for the 50K version of the Vermont 50 Bike and Run. Oh yes! And so I did register and began to make plans for Sue Ellen and I to visit old haunts; following my race participation of course. And the dreams began, as so many dreams of running and finishing ultras have begun, of having a day to run around and through and up and down the backroads and single-track trails of beautiful Vermont. My fantasies!

There was a problem, however. The problem was the progression of age-related deterioration of skills. Stuff happens after sixty and "stuff" really happens after seventy. "Why don't my legs move easily when I run?" "Why is there no spring in my step?" "Why do I go splat when I fall instead of a tumble?" "What has happened to my balance?" "Why do I go so slow?" I know, of course, but this reality is not recognized in my dreams. What is recognized is the broken hip I experienced from a fall on the Appalachian Trail portion of the JFK 50 miler a couple of years ago. Amazing how that experience makes one more cautious over rocks and roots.

All of this and following a succession of DNFs due to failure to make time cutoffs, had led to my "self-declaration" that there would be no more ultras for me (other than the twenty-four-hour variety where you run as far as you wish/can within twenty-four hours and no dreaded time cutoffs!). Yes, no more! I now understood my limitations. Yes! But then here I was standing at the starting line of the Vermont 50K on September 30, 2018. What was I thinking?

Now I have to say again, that my experience of crewing for my son at the 100-mile event had shown me what a friendly and super well-organized event this was. And this 50 mile/50K variety was no different. I can only highly recommend it. And the weather for this year was perfect. The forties in the morning and the fifties in the afternoon, and dry. Perfect. There was only one "glitch" in my understanding of the listed time cutoffs. As a back-of-the-pack runner for the past twenty years and one continually stressed by making time cutoffs, I was really concerned about the apparent tight cutoff times allowed for the late aid stations. The times allowed to move from one station to another seemed to be well beyond my ability to achieve. With this in mind, I had no real expectations of finishing and had convinced myself to just have a "taste" of Vermont. And a "taste" is what I had. There was only one aid station that allowed crew access for the 50K (other than the last station, 2.5 miles from the finish) and that was at 13.5 miles. I thought that with a "good day" I could be allowed to get that far. I would meet Sue Ellen and be happy with the "Vermont half." The problem was, however, that I arrived at that aid station two and a half hours ahead of time! Why? I was practically the last 50K runner and yet arrived at a mid-way aid station two and a half hours ahead of time. Why? Sue Ellen was not expecting me and the problem was that there was no way at this aid station to know if a certain runner had gone through or not. I was perplexed because I felt good, but then I knew there would be lots of climbing ahead and then those increasingly difficult time cut-offs! I stood around for a half-hour until I discovered Sue Ellen waiting in a parking lot and confirmed that I would drop. With no way of knowing my status should I go on, and no way for Sue Ellen to meet me at an aid station where I could not arrive in time to make the cutoff time, it was "best" to accept the "Vermont half" and be happy with a beautiful day running up and over Vermont mountains and running by beautiful farms and pastures. And it was special!

But as I look back at my misinterpretation of those aid station time cutoffs I can realize something different from my previous twenty years of ultra experience. The difference was that this event was not just a 50K run nor even a run combined with a 50-mile component: it also had mountain bike varieties as well. And if we look at the over-all time allowed to complete the 50K component (ten and a half hours), perhaps the late time cutoffs were actually more generous than I had thought at the time. I was just not used to this aspect of scheduling aid station time cut-offs in a run/bike event.

So what is the message of this "report?" Well first and foremost, I can highly recommend the Vermont ultra races! They are friendly, super well-organized, and super well-supported by lots and lots of friendly and helpful volunteers. And yes, the course is beautiful and everything I had dreamed about. But there it is again, dreams versus reality. Why can't I just say no! Why can't I accept my limitations? Why can't I be thankful and happy with my past opportunities (which I am!)? Why can't I just say no! And why am I even thinking of running next year?

Jack Andrish
October 1, 2018

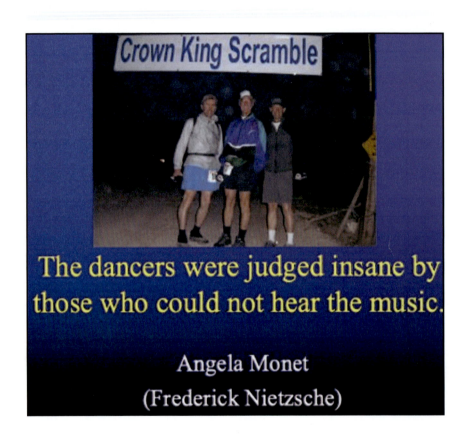

Poems, Reflections, and Other Stuff

My first exposure to a 100 miler was with the Western States 100. I had tried to enter myself, but was not accepted in the lottery. My son, however, got accepted and I agreed (jumped at the chance really) to serve as his crew. It was a thrilling and at the same time a scary experience. My son had recruited a pacer, but when his pacer opted out at mile 62, I alone was left to be his pacer. That meant I had to run 38 miles and I was not prepared. But running with him through the night and into the day was a transformative experience. I was in awe of his commitment to finish; and finish he did. The next day as I flew home while still emotionally high from the experience, I composed a poem which attempted to illustrate my feelings. I challenged myself to be a pacer and I was so proud of my son's accomplishment as well as all of those runners who got to the starting line.

July 2000

Pacers Have Feelings Too

THE PREAMBLE:
A jog, a run
Fantastic fun
Adrenaline charged with GU
A hill, a stream
Inspires a dream
To cover the planet's hue
We start with small
And mask our gall
By running a 10K through
But as we stride
Into the tide
Of the ever increasing few
We look to find
The *ultimate* kind
To challenge our forefoot two
And there we mate
The Western States
With our dreams of glory for me and for you
The Western States
The Western States
The land of green, brown, and blue
The Western States
The Western States
For moments of pleasure and rue
Alas a fly
In the ointment, my
Skills are not equal to you
And reality shows
In the after glows
Of the difference we always knew
So it's you that applied
And it's me that's denied
And I sleep with my dreams anew

But my awe of you fountains
As your training climbs mountains
While your body form functions as new
What a glorious goal
To prepare for the role
Of a runner the "States" will woo
But not to be outcast
My plight becomes forecast
As the role of pacer and crew
The role of pacer and crew
The role of pacer and crew
Although not complete
In my grasp of the feat
I prepare to be pacer and crew
I prepare to be pacer and crew
I prepare to be pacer and crew
I train as I'm able
To run and set table
I prepare to be pacer and crew

THE TRIP AND CHECK-IN:

Oh glorious Tahoe
Oh scenic Squaw Valley
We're here for the tried and the true
The check-in is seamless
For the teams and the teamless
To enroll and to flow into queue
There are meetings for racers
But no listings for pacers
The agenda is clearly for you
There are sessions for crewers
For don't and for doers
But no mention of pacers to be or taboo
The message delivered
I should have endeavored
To better consider this too
The pacer is there for support
The pacer is not to report
The pacer is selfless
And preferably faceless
The pacer is only for you
Conceived out of need
But confused as a weed
The pacer is only for you

THE RUN:

Oh wonderful day
'Fore the Sun's first ray
The start of the "States" is ado
Of all training
And all feigning
The day of all days will ensue
"My runner" is golden
A sight to beholden
As emotion implanted and grew
A tear swells inside me
As runners go by me
Amidst cheers and photo-ops too
A moment in passing
As crowds are amassing
I remember my duties as pacer and crew
I honor my duties as pacer and crew
I fly to my Jeep
To pay homage and weep
For "success to my runner" is our mantra and glue
Success to my runner
I must meet my runner
I must provide comfort and GU
I must not be late
For each possible gate
That allows me the chance to support and to coo
My runner implodes
After suffering loads
From the heat of the canyon's flue
El Dorado engages
Devil's Thumb's rages
Bringing down my runner's fiber and glue
But courage wills out
As my runner is stout
On to the forest and view!

And now my role switches
From crew into paces
For on-line support to pull through
Into the dimness
And down through the rimless
Pathways of clutter that lead to the dew
The night is surreal
With flashlights we deal
My code for my runner will lighten our view
I help and encourage
Console, not discourage
My feat as the pacer knows how to subdue
The river in splendor
Will sooth and will render
Refresh and renew, our spirit is true
My place as a pacer
Rests back of the racer
Our role is support just for you
At check-ins and stations
We pacers of nations
Know how to subside from the crew
We stand and befriend
The help from a hand
That nourishes our runner anew
A glorious night
A glorious sight
Our runner survives and moves on and into
But wait just a moment
Our pacer's in torment
As mile after mile are extracting their due
Pacer miles cleared
Run 38 neared
With pain and fatigue gasping through
The finish approaches
Midst cheers, no reproaches
My runner, my hero, for me and for you
Engulfed by respect

And surrounded by deft
Attention, my runner adorns the respect of the crew
The pacer meanwhile
Is left to de-file
And stand all-alone with his stiff and sore too
The pacer is solely
Intent to be wholly
Support and subside from all view
But Pacers have feelings too
Pacers have feelings too
Exhaust and fatigue
Inherit this steed
And Pacers have feelings too

Jack Andrish

EPILOGUE: The Morning After

My runner, my racer, my fun
My hero, my comrade, my son
Emotions of pride for *all* runners *who tried*
This test of one's courage
Intent to discourage
But at the completion
No cowards exist.
At the completion
No cowards exist.

An Ultra Marathoner's Journey

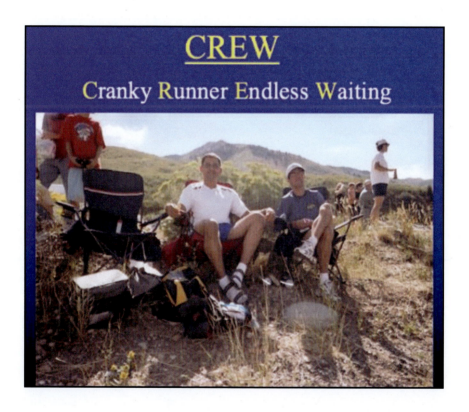

Shadows

Shadows don't lie.
Shadows follow us through life with relentless accuracy.
I run.
In my mind's eye, I run with the wind at my back on winged feet.
I run with an effortless skill and grace that only the gifted possess.
In my mind's eye.
I run.
I spot my shadow. Not my shadow! No!
That shadow looks old. Bent. Crooked, even!
I run.
I try not to look at my shadow.

Jack Andrish
November 2006

I Run Because I Can.

I run because I can.
I run because there still exists a small glow of youth somewhere in my brain.
I run because of green days and black nights.
I run because I can.
I run because to not run would be to leave the last remnant of my youth,
Alone.
I run because I watch my granddaughter take her first steps,
Quickly, without fear, with a future full of opportunities.
I run because I can.
I run because of rain that blankets my face and renews my senses.
I run because to not run would be tantamount to giving up.
I run because of comrades and camaraderie.
I run because of rocky trails and pine needles; enchanting meadows and purple peaks.
I run because I can.
I run because running is my link with a time when my feet were light and my legs were strong and my balance was like the cat.
I run because I can.
I run because of the anticipation that my legs will once again be strong and my feet will be light.
I run because of hope.
I run because to not run would mean to abdicate the thrill of anticipation.
I run because I can.

Jack Andrish
November 2006

Jack Andrish

Reflections on the MMT 100: or Life from the Blue Tees

I used to be a golfer. Actually, for most of my life I was a very good golfer and as such, I always preferred to play from the championship "blue tees." After all, the true test was to play the course at its maximum length. Sure, playing from the white tees could cut a few strokes off my score; but that was not the same. That would not feel quite as good as playing from the blues, even if my score was higher. Golf is a test and I preferred to make it the best test.

I started college as a future engineer. It was certainly a demanding curriculum and I was okay with it. But I discovered the possibility of becoming a doctor and at the time, going to medical school was another way to play from the blue tees. And so I did and then went on to choose a residency. The choices were basically a "medical" specialty or a surgical specialty. I chose surgery; not because I was destined to be a surgeon, but because to me, at the time, surgery represented the blue tees. It would stretch my limits and anything else would be playing from the white tees. I chose orthopaedics because I enjoyed the "mechanics" of it and the colleagues within the specialty. It was great fun. After residency, I chose to do a fellowship in pediatric orthopaedics at the A.I. duPont Institute in Wilmington, Delaware. Thereafter, I chose an academic career and was lucky enough to return to the Cleveland Clinic. Academic medicine, again, was to me playing from the blue tees. My practice was divided between sports medicine, research in knee ligament injury, and pediatric orthopaedics. In my pediatric orthopaedic practice I chose to include surgery for the correction of spinal deformity. I worked very hard to be a good scoliosis surgeon, not because it came easy to me (because it didn't), but because to me that was playing from the blue tees.

And so, as I reflect upon my recent experience on Massanutten Mountain, unsuccessfully trying to complete the 100-mile distance over this very rocky and demanding course, I ask myself "why?" Why Massanutten and for how long? The "why" is easy, of course. Accepting the challenge of the MMT 100, just as accepting the challenge of Leadville, or Wasatch, or Western States, is to play from the blue tees! The "for how long" is a more difficult question. Just as I try not to look at my shadow, the shadow of an old man, I try not to consider or plan for the white tees of ultra running. But the day will come, I know. And if I am lucky, I will still be able to continue to enjoy the people and the sport as much as I do now, and from the white tees.

Jack Andrish
May 27, 2007

That Special Run

What defines a good run? Is it a run where personal bests are achieved? Is it a run where our feet are light? Is it a run where nothing hurts? Of course a good run can be any or all of those things. But a good run also can be age dependent and as I enter the geriatric age (officially) I find that none of the above applies. It always hurts. Personal bests are way behind me. And light of foot? Ha! No, while going for a run tonight and trying to beat an oncoming rainstorm, I found the answer. Running through our "Metro Park" and descending through (note the verb "descending!") a snow field at dusk with fog rising off the patches of snow, I spontaneously incanted "Thank you Lord. Thank you for the privilege to have one more run, one more run through a favorite space in my special place. Thank you for this day and this 'good run.'"

Jack Andrish
February 11, 2009

The Last Run

When will it come? How will I know it? I may be experiencing, the experience.

Jack Andrish
March 2009

Embrace the Moment

Embrace the moment when nothing hurts and movement flows
Embrace the moment when there are no limits
Embrace the moment of youth
Embrace the moment
Embrace the moment when pain succumbs to whatever it is that allows the momentary peace
Embrace the moment when movement rules and overcomes the rigor of age
Embrace the moment that pleases and redefines our purpose
Embrace the moment that allows a fellowship with friends
Embrace the moment of sharing with family
Embrace the moment in time

February 2010

Don't Give Up on Dreams

Don't give up on dreams.
Don't let the naysayers let you believe that you no longer can believe.
Don't give up on dreams.
Dreams inspire
Dreams desire
Dreams require hope and hope requires belief that "I can!"
Don't give up on dreams.
How many times have I crossed the American River at the Rucky Chucky crossing?
How many times?
In my dreams.
Don't take that away from me.
I won't let that slip away from me.
I won't give up on my dreams.

Jack Andrish
June 28, 2010

Who is that Man?

Who is that man in the picture? Me? No, it couldn't be me. I know I'm not that young anymore, but I'm not old. But I look old; old! When did that happen? I have fantasized about being that old man who still can run 100 miles or play golf in the seventies. I fantasized that I would be old yet able to compete. People would say, "Look at that old man and what he can still do!" But in my fantasy I would look old, but somehow, not. Not like this. Not bent and lined. Not a scraggly gray beard. Where is the paradox here? I should be happy and reassured that I am indeed old and still able to ski and run and golf. And not just ski, but ski the backcountry. And not just run, but run trails and ultras. And golf, well not everything in my fantasy is real. But the pictures! Why do the pictures give a different tale? What is real? My fantasy or the pictures?

Who is that man and when did it happen?

Jack Andrish
August 28, 2011

Within or Without

We've heard that perception is reality, but whose perception? There is the perception we have within us. And there is the perception held by those around us. Are both of equal importance? Are both real? Which one do we believe when there is conflict?

There is a view within us that is not always true. There is a view about us that is not always true. How can we know which view to follow?

I wish I knew.

Jack Andrish
August 5, 2012

The Finish Line

I took one step closer to a finish line today: one step closer.
One week ago I had stepped onto this trail with anticipation and expectation.
I was one step closer to a finish line.
As I run past the spot where an aid station was positioned, I remember the cheers of encouragement and the soft eyes of empathy.
I was one step closer.
But I was not to see a finish line that day.
I was one step closer, but not enough: again.
It was good, today, to be back on the trail; back on the trail with dreams of preparing, again, to get one step closer to a finish line.
Of course we have our limits. We have human limits that change over time.
But what are those limits? How could we know our limits unless we continue to test them; over and over?
How do we know when a finish line will finally appear; or *the* finish line ends it all?
We can't.
Do we really wish to meet the finish line by default?
Today it was good to be back and one step closer.
One step closer to a finish line!

Jack Andrish
August 4, 2012

Dreams
To Dream or Not to Dream

It seems as I reminisce over my folder of poems and other thoughts, that I have a fixation on dreams. When do dreams become a reality? When do dreams cease to be possible?

When do we become foolish to dream? When do we look like fools to follow our dreams? When should we stop dreaming?

I still do not know the answer; or maybe it is that I know, but do not want to recognize the answer. Probably that. I know, I just do not wish to know. Life is fulfilling when we dream and work toward making our dreams come true. The journey, after all, is the dream, not the finish line. What comes after the finish line? Nothing? Another finish line after finish line after finish line? No, it is the journey to the finish line that keeps us dreaming.

So when are our dreams wrong? Probably not when the only one responsible and accountable is ourselves. But when our dreams adversely affect others, especially our loved ones, then maybe that is when it is time to dream another dream. So it is okay to abandon our dreams? If our dreams make others sad, then yes. Stop the dream! But if there is a comfort in this, it could be that to stop one dream does not mean we have to stop all dreaming. It is just hard. Hard to stop when something in us keeps telling us that the journey is still worth it. That it still may be possible, if all the stars line up and all of our physical and mental shortcomings and frailties somehow are overcome; overcome for that one last journey to the finish line. One last mystical experience.

I think I'll continue to dream.

Jack Andrish
2014

Growing Old

Why is it that the mind still has us young, and the mirror sees us old? Why is it that each morning when we awaken and start the day, our body feels old and stiff and weak, but moments later, not much later really, when our minds are fully awake, we are back to thinking of ourselves as young? Young without limits. Young with unthinkable balance and strength and endurance! Young with feet that can lightly skip over rocky and rooty trails with only the occasional trip; a trip that is followed by a graceful tuck-and-roll. Why is it? Why is it that there is a conflict between the mind and the body? Which do we believe, the mind or the body? Which should we believe? I suppose we should believe the body because that is what we can see. We can feel. We can understand. The mind is more difficult. Does the mind follow the body or the body follow the mind? I think it is the latter. Or at least I would like to dream that it is the latter. What do pictures show? Really! They don't show the mind. Or maybe they do. We can see the mind in someone's eyes. Eyes still filled with hopes and dreams, or eyes blurred by defeat and resignation.

So maybe it is time for me to resign from my dreams that are no longer attainable. That will be easier on my family. And maybe easier on me too. Maybe it is time for me to listen to my body; for sure my body is trying to tell me! But then there is the mind. The kernel of a dream that still exists. I just can't stop the dream.

Jack Andrish
2014

When Racing Becomes the Fun Run

I have always wondered about the term "fun run." What, really is "fun" about running? Certainly getting up early to run before work or even late in the evening after a long day of work cannot always be considered as "fun." Those runs are more often efforts to gain or maintain a certain level of conditioning. Yes, "efforts." And running in a "race" to the point of exhaustion and metabolic chaos cannot always be considered as "fun." But then, there is the fun of training for an upcoming race; imagining the thrill of anticipation and the exhilaration of the finish! Yes, "imagining" these things are often more "fun" than the execution.

That said, I have been lucky enough to have experienced the thrill of anticipation and the exhilaration of the finish, but at the expense of always racing to make the time cut-offs. And all too often, failing to make a time cut-off. I am and have always been, a "back-of-the-packer."

But now in my years of diminishing skills, I have finally understood what is a "fun run." No matter the distance traveled, any distance can be a "fun run" if the pace allows it. It is, after all, all about pace. By eliminating the element of "time limits," we can have "fun" for any distance; 3 miles or 30 miles! It makes no difference if the pace allows us to maintain the "fun" of the experience. And it can!

And so, I have finally accepted and understood that I can make my own "race," for fun. Or, I can enter an "official" race and go, for "fun," as far as the time limits allow. No pressure, just the thrill of running at the best pace I can, for "fun." Wow! It has only taken me seventy-two years to discover the truth of a "fun run."

Jack Andrish
August 2016

When "Do-Overs" are Over

A wonderful thing about "do-overs," they can keep us going and validate our failures and mistakes. We DNF and understand that "next year" we will train better and do better. That gives us inspiration and motivation to extend "the thrill of anticipation" for yet another year. We still have potential! But what happens when we come to realize that our time has come and gone for "do-overs?" When do we finally realize that our diminishing skills are finally going to eliminate the "do-over?" When? How? Why?

Well, for me the time has come. But it has not come easily. It is hard and even painful to finally give up on the dance that is the participation in ultra races. For me, this process of acceptance has taken almost ten years. Life puts a continuing series of obstacles in our path; age and an ever increasing and persistent series of injury and diminishing skill. How is it that my times have continued to spiral downward? Why can't I maintain a reasonable leg turnover? Why is my balance diminishing and my fear of falling, increasing? Oh, I know why. The culprit is age. So much in life is under our control, but so much is not and the progressive impairments and ailments that come with advancing age are, yes, inevitable. Tough to accept, but accept we must.

And so I have come to realize that technical trails are only for me to hike and not run. And ultra "races" are out because I don't need one more DNF due to failure to make a time cutoff to convince me. But the good news is that we may not get "do-overs" as we once did, but we can make our own transition into a gentler form of "ultra." We can even make our own self-made ultras (with a modified definition of "ultra" distance). Sure, this way we can still have the "thrill of anticipation." We can even have another "mystical experience" that comes with extreme (to be defined by self) endurance and by "running" through the night.

And I also recognize that even by this modified definition of "ultra running," the end will come. But until that time, I can be thankful for whatever I can do, in whatever way I can do it. And appreciate that with this understanding, I may once again be able to experience the "thrill of anticipation."

Jack Andrish
March 2017

I Watch Them Run

I watch them run; the young. I watch them glide with seemingly an effortless grace. I watch them run with long strides that I now only view as myself in my dreams. I am envious. The reality of my age-dependent decline is now all too real. My ability to deny is no longer even a bit legitimate. I have tried to deny for many years now, but each year cements the reality. A decade or two ago I had listened to a scholarly lecture by an exercise physiologist in which he described the "inevitable" arrival of the "metabolic cliff." The "cliff" describes the obligatory marked decline of aerobic and musculoskeletal capacity that occurs by the age of seventy-five. Prior to "the cliff" we can positively alter the obligatory downward slope of metabolic function by pursuing regular aerobic and strength training exercise. The slope is still increasingly downward in the fifties and sixties, but we can reduce the slope. Following "the cliff" however, we are doomed to a progression of diminishing skills. At the time I listened to this lecture, age seventy-five seemed a very long time from where I was. It was abstract. But time has passed and I am now off the "cliff" and watching the young with envy. Once my legs felt strong and my step felt light and secure. I do remember the feeling that the young runner feels. But I doubt that he understands the ephemeral nature of his experience. Someday he will reach "the cliff." Someday his stride will shorten and his legs will stiffen and his balance will suffer. And someday that young runner will experience what we all, who are fortunate enough to live long enough, experience. Sadness for the loss is also part of the experience arriving at "the cliff." But thankfulness that once we were that young runner and thankful that we took advantage of the opportunity to glide through a run and enjoy the thrill of accomplishment.

    Jack Andrish
    January 20, 2019

In My Dreams

In my dreams.
In my dreams I can run
In my dreams I can run with joy and agility
In my dreams I can run over rocky trails and slippery roots
In my dreams I can take my place at the starting line of the Western States 100
In my dreams I can run
But all dreams have an ending
All dreams end with awakening and reality
All dreams, at some point, end

Jack Andrish
February 2020

The "Real" Runner

I have often been referred to as a "runner." I still cringe when this happens. I run, but I never have considered myself to be a "real" runner. I would be somewhat embarrassed if someone called me that. My son is a "real runner," my daughter is a "real runner," and my wife was once a "real runner." But not me. I have tried mightily over my life to be a "real runner." As a youth I would practice endlessly at a local track to improve my speed. I would try many types of form and gait. I would toe-in, I would toe-out, I would toe straight ahead. I would try intervals. I would try a form of plyometrics (although of course at that time I had no idea what plyometrics were; I would just practice jumping). I tried sprinting. I tried distance running. I was just never able to be a "real runner."

So what then defines a "real runner?" In my mind that had meant speed. And of course that can be one aspect of a definition. But then as I entered my thirties and forties and found that I didn't have to be the fastest runner to participate, my own definition of the "real runner" became a bit more inclusive. "If you call it a run, then it is a run." Let's face it, we can have "real fast runners" and "real slow runners" and all of those in between. And you know what? At least in the ultra running community, we are all "real runners!"

January 2020

Deceptions

Memories. We most often love them. But memories can be deceptive. For instance, there was a period of time about twelve to fifteen years ago that I was enamored by the thought of crossing Hope Pass, TWICE, while attempting the Leadville Trail 100. I ran that course four times (three times while attempting the race and once during a Leadville Training Camp). Four times! Three times during the day and once during the night. I wouldn't say that I loved the entire course, but there was a section that I loved. It was magical and just what we would always dream of running; runnable single track circling a traverse around the base of Mt. Elbert amongst a beautiful forest. I had always wanted to share that experience with Sue Ellen, to show her this mystical section of trail. Access to the trail going "out" was from a trail head at Half Moon camping area. I remembered it well: turn left then right and then access that beautiful runnable trail. What a relief after struggling through the first 30-plus miles, most recently on an exposed road section. What a relief to finally get back on a trail! And a magical trail section through a mystical mountain forest.

Okay, enough of that. This week while visiting Sean in Frisco, Colorado, we traveled back to Half Moon and set up a camp. Perhaps the first deception of my memory was just the car ride to Half Moon. I hadn't remembered how much up-hill that dirt road section had. We (myself, Sue Ellen, Sean, and my two granddaughters Kaitlin and Allison) then hiked about Mt. Massive. The next day was to be a hike on that "magical/mystical" trail section around Mt. Elbert. At last I would have a chance to show Sue Ellen my favorite trail section of the Leadville Trail 100 (Sean and my granddaughters would go on to summit Mt. Elbert). I was so excited. But almost immediately I became confused. The trail was not relatively gentle. It was a rocky/rooty CLIMB. Rocky and rooty and persistent climbing was NOT what I remembered. "We must have missed the Colorado Trail section that traversed around Mt. Elbert leading to Twin Lakes." In fact, after climbing for a mile I insisted that we descend back to the trail head and look for the trail I remembered. We did, but after discussing my dilemma with some back-packers, I accepted the fact that I must have been wrong with my memory. We went back to the climb and this time after well-over a mile of a rocky/rooty climb, we found the section of the Colorado Trail that I remembered so fondly. It was beautiful. It was very runnable. It was magical.

So what is my take on this experience? As with most of our ultra running experiences, there is pain at the time, but it is the magical/mystical experiences we remember, not the pain. Isn't that great!

Jack Andrish
July 2020